Arden of Faversham

NEW MERMAIDS

General editor: Brian Gibbons
Professor of English Literature, University of Münster

Previous general editors
Philip Brockbank
Brian Morris
Roma Gill

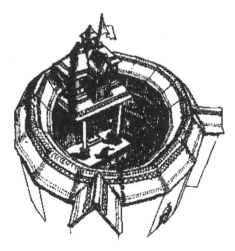

Reconstruction of an Elizabethan theatre
stage by C. Walter Hodges

NEW MERMAIDS

The Alchemist
All for Love
Arden of Faversham
The Atheist's Tragedy
Bartholmew Fair
The Beaux' Stratagem
The Broken Heart
Bussy D'Ambois
The Changeling
A Chaste Maid in Cheapside
The Country Wife
The Critic
The Double-Dealer
Dr Faustus
The Duchess of Malfi
The Dutch Courtesan
Eastward Ho!
Edward the Second
Epicoene or The Silent Woman
Every Man In His Humour
Gammer Gurton's Needle
An Ideal Husband
The Importance of Being Earnest
The Jew of Malta
The Knight of the Burning Pestle
Lady Windermere's Fan
London Assurance
Love for Love
The Malcontent
The Man of Mode
Marriage A-la-Mode

A New Way to Pay Old Debts
The Old Wife's Tale
The Plain Dealer
The Playboy of the Western World
The Provoked Wife
The Recruiting Officer
The Relapse
The Revenger's Tragedy
The Rivals
The Roaring Girl
The Rover
The School for Scandal
She Stoops to Conquer
The Shoemaker's Holiday
The Spanish Tragedy
Tamburlaine
Three Late Medieval Morality Plays
    Mankind
    Everyman
    Mundus et Infans
Thyestes
'Tis Pity She's a Whore
Volpone
The Way of the World
The White Devil
The Witch
The Witch of Edmonton
A Woman Killed with Kindness
A Woman of No Importance
Women Beware Women

Arden's House today. Arden was murdered in the ground-floor room in the centre of the photograph. (Photo: Martin White)

NEW MERMAIDS

Arden of Faversham

edited by **Martin White**

Senior Lecturer in Drama
University of Bristol

A & C Black • London
W W Norton • New York

Reprinted 1990, 1993, 1995, 1997, 2000
by A & C Black (Publishers) Limited
35 Bedford Row, London WC1R 4JH
ISBN 0-7136-3295-X

First New Mermaid edition 1982
by Ernest Benn Limited

Published in the United States of America
by W. W. Norton & Company Inc.
500 Fifth Avenue, New York, N.Y. 10110
ISBN 0-393-95236-3

A CIP catalogue record for this book
is available from the British Library and
the Library of Congress.

Printed in Great Britain by
Whitstable Printers Ltd,
Whitstable, Kent

CONTENTS

ACKNOWLEDGEMENTS

I AM PARTICULARLY grateful to Mr M.P. Jackson for access to his Oxford B. Litt. thesis 'Material for an edition of *Arden of Feversham*' (1963), and I should also like to acknowledge the debt I owe to M.L. Wine's stimulating and scholarly edition in the Revels series (1973).

I have been fortunate enough to direct the play twice — at the University Theatre, Manchester, in 1975, and at the Edinburgh Festival in 1978 — and I should like to thank those concerned for giving me the opportunity to learn about the play in performance.

I am also grateful to Philip Roberts for his initial encouragement and continued interest; to Oliver Neville for his comments on the Introduction; to Brian Gibbons, who saved me from making many an error; and, above all, to Julia Hills for her constant support and help.

LIST OF ABBREVIATIONS

ed.	editor
n.	note
O.E.D.	*Oxford English Dictionary*
Q1	First Quarto 1592
Q2	Second Quarto 1599
Q3	Third Quarto 1633
Qq	the first three quartos (Q1, Q2, Q3)
s.d.	stage direction
s.h.	speech heading
Adams	H. H. Adams, *English Domestic Or, Homiletic Tragedy 1575 to 1642*, New York, 1943.
Bluestone	Max Bluestone, 'The Imagery of Tragic Melodrama In *Arden of Feversham*', in M. Bluestone and N. Rabkin (eds.), *Shakespeare's Contemporaries*, Second Edition, New Jersey, 1970. Reprinted from *Drama Survey*, Vol. 5 (1966), 171–81.
Chapman	Raymond Chapman, '*Arden of Faversham*: Its Interest Today' *English*, XI (1956), 15–17.
Cust	Lionel Cust, '*Arden of Feversham*', *Archaeologica Cantiana*, XXXIV (1920), 101–126.
Holinshed	Ralph Holinshed, *The Chronicles of England, Scotland, and Ireland*, 2nd edition, 1587.
Jackson	M. P. Jackson, 'Material for an edition of *Arden of Feversham*', unpubl. B. Litt. thesis, Oxford, 1963.
Johnson	Samuel Johnson, *A Dictionary of the English Language*, 1755.
Ousby	Ian Ousby and Heather Dubrow Ousby, 'Art and Language in *Arden of Faversham*', *Durham University Journal*, Vol. LXVIII 1, (New Series Vol. XXXVII No. 1), December 1975, 47–54.
Sugden	E. H. Sugden, *A Topographical Dictionary to the Works of Shakespeare and His Fellow Dramatists*, 1925.
Tilley	M. P. Tilley, *A Dictionary of the Proverbs in England in the Sixteenth and Seventeenth Centuries*, Ann Arbor, 1950.
Youngblood	Sarah Youngblood, 'Theme and Imagery in *Arden of Feversham*', *Studies in English Literature*, III (1963), 207–218.

INTRODUCTION

DATE AND SOURCES

'THE TRAGEDIE of Arden of Feuersham & blackwill' was entered in the Stationer's Register on 3 April 1592, and was published in the same year by Edward White. Allowance for a period of time during which the play was performed prior to publication suggests, therefore, that a slightly earlier date might be established as the upper limit for the play's composition.

The principal source for *Arden* is the version of the story given in Holinshed's *Chronicles,* first published in 1577. M. L. Wine has suggested (pp. xl–xli), however, that certain moments in the play appear to be inspired not by the narrative itself but by the marginal glosses added to the second edition published in 1587.

If this suggestion is accepted, it is possible to narrow the period during which the play was written to between 1587/8 and 1591/2, but in the absence of further firm evidence a more precise date cannot be determined.

The playwright's handling of his major source demonstrates his certainty of purpose and his artistic and technical skill in achieving his aims. Although he follows the narrative line of the *Chronicles* fairly closely (even, at times, repeating it verbatim), he diverges from, or adds to, Holinshed's narrative in a number of ways, elaborating on and clarifying certain of the murder attempts (in Scenes III, IX, and XII, for example), and using the unfolding of the murder story to provide not only narrative tension, but also a framework within which to explore the development of his characters' minds and relationships.

In his treatment of the three main protagonists in particular, the playwright's intention is clearly to complicate their personalities by strengthening and underlining the contradictions within them, an approach which contributes greatly to the impression of realism in the character portrayal so frequently commented on by critics of the play. The playwright is also concerned to balance the characters with each other so that none appears more or less sympathetic or culpable than another.

He omits, for example, Holinshed's information that although Arden knew of his wife's adultery with Mosby, 'bicause he would not offend hir, and so loose the benefit which he hoped to gaine at some of hir freends in bearing with hir lewdnesse... he was contented to winke at hir filthie disorder'. Symonds argues that the omission of this motive 'enfeebles the dramatic Arden' because it alone makes Arden's 'contemptible compliance intelligible',[1] but to have included it (as Adams points out),[2] would have made Arden guilty of a mortal sin from the outset, which would have prevented the playwright from concentrating on the immorality of Arden's public actions. The dramatist's awareness of the degree of hostility towards the character that these public actions would arouse in the audience probably accounts for his decision to leave out other examples of Arden's covetousness found in Holinshed, such as the fact that Arden had arranged for the annual fair of St Valentine to be held entirely on his land 'so reaping all the gaines to himselfe, and bereauing the towne of that portion which was woont to come to the inhabitants'. In addition, by making Arden's attitude to Alice less explicable, the character is made more complex and interesting (see p. xxiii).

After the murder (according to Holinshed), while Arden's corpse was still concealed in the house, Alice 'caused hir daughter to plaie on the virginals, and they dansed, and she with them',[3] after which she suggested that to while away the time they should 'plaie a game at the tables', where, of course, Arden had been stabbed and bludgeoned to death only minutes before. The playwright probably omitted these potentially striking theatrical moments (displaying, it should be noted, a determination to control his material and audience response that totally belies the tone of the title-page), in order to prevent Alice, too, from becoming so extreme in her behaviour that she would lose credibility as a character and the equilibrium of the play be destroyed.

The dramatist has, however, skilfully integrated into other moments of the action the element of brazen recklessness in Alice that these incidents suggest: for example, when she takes the business with the poisoned broth further than she need (I, 386–9), or tries too hard to persuade Arden to stay (I, 397–403), and even, possibly, in her direct 'challenge' to the audience in her speeches at I, 93–104 and XIV, 142–153.

The most extensive changes made by the playwright in the characters he took from Holinshed concern Michael (who he develops into a man torn between his conscience, his fears, and his desires),[4] and Mosby, who figures less, and is presented more favourably in the source than in the play.

---

[1] J.A. Symonds, *Shakespere's Predecessors in the English Drama* (1900), p. 353.
[2] Adams, p. 104.
[3] See I, 220–1 and n.
[4] See particularly IV, 58–86 and n.

Holinshed describes Mosby as a 'tailor by occupation, a blacke swart man, seruant to the Lord North', but makes no mention of his social climbing; in Holinshed, Arden was many times 'greatlie prouoked by Mosbie to fight with him, but he would not', whereas the play presents Mosby as the coward; according to the *Chronicles* Mosby at first refused to have any part in the 'cowardlie' method by which it was proposed to murder Arden 'but in a furie floong awaie', being won round only after Alice 'fell downe vpon hir knees to him, and besought him to go through with the matter'. In the play, of course, the murder plan is all Mosby's idea.

Comparison of play and source also reveals the dramatist's skill in creating powerful scenes both from his own imagination (such as the scenes in the mist with the ferryman, or the confrontation between Alice and Mosby in Scene VIII), and from factual details in the source (the encounter between Reede and Arden in Scene XIII, for example).

The comparison also illustrates the playwright's awareness of the requirements of a play to be performed as opposed to a prose narrative to be read, and his technical skill in meeting these demands is convincing evidence that whoever wrote this play had direct, practical experience of the theatre. He creates the character of Franklin to solve certain dramatic problems (see below, p. xx); he merges the figures of Alice's maid and Mosby's sister into the single role of Susan; he replaces the grocers Prune and Cole, who were (according to Holinshed) Alice's dinner guests on the night of the murder, with Bradshaw and Adam Fowle; and he makes it possible to double the part of Bradshaw with Lord Cheiny, and that of Clarke with Reede.

The playwright also condenses episodes in Holinshed in the interests of dramatic economy. For example, the incidents that make up Scene II (the hiring of Black Will and Shakebag by Greene, and the giving of the incriminating letter to Bradshaw), extend in the source over a longer period of time, and occur in more than one place. In addition to compressing this into one scene, the playwright takes the opportunity to introduce Shakebag (who, overall, plays a much less emphatic role in Holinshed), and then develops the character in tandem with Black Will.

The story of the murder of Thomas Arden caught and held the public imagination for decades after it was committed and was frequently referred to. The dramatist, however, appears to have relied solely on Holinshed for the details, and he displays no knowledge of the account of the murder and trial contained in the Faversham Wardmote Book.[5]

[5] See Wine, pp. 160–3 for the Wardmote Book account.

Finally, although the similarities between Greene's attack on Arden's rapaciousness (I, 474 – 77), and lines from Robert Crowley's pamphlet, *The Way to Wealth*,[6] have been pointed out before,[7] there are further indications of the playwright's direct use of this pamphlet, the implications of which are discussed more fully below (see pp. xviii–xx).

The lines which compare with Greene's come from the opening section of the pamphlet where Crowley sets out the answer he supposes a poor man would give if asked to name 'What thinge he thinketh to be the cause of sedition'. The answer takes the form of a diatribe against covetous landlords, at the end of which Crowley responds: 'Alasse, poore man, it pitieth me to see the myserable estate that thou arte in!',[8] which compares closely with Alice's response to Greene's speech:

Alas, poor gentleman, I pity you,
And woe is me that any man should want.

                                        (I, 483 – 4)

In the light of this, it is interesting to note that throughout this opening section Crowley frequently uses the image of the 'unweeded land' which is, of course, a common Renaissance figure for the disordered state, but one which is, significantly, also found frequently in *Arden*.

AUTHORSHIP

Although critical praise for *Arden of Faversham* is almost unanimous, no such consensus of opinion exists on the vexed question of the authorship. Over the years, prompted by the play's undoubted quality, there has been no shortage of critics prepared to try to identify the playwright, despite S.P. Sherman's Cassandra-like warning that the 'scholar who commits himself on the authorship of an anonymous old play takes his life in his hands',[9] and the list of names proposed ranges from well-known dramatists such as Greene and Peele to frankly eccentric suggestions such as Lord Oxford or the 6th Earl of Derby.[10]

[6]   Robert Crowley, *The Way To Wealth,* Early English Text Society, Extra Series, No. XV (1872), 129 – 50.

[7]   Chapman, p. 15; Wine, p. lxiii.

[8]   Crowley, op.cit., pp. 132 – 3.

[9]   S.P. Sherman, quoted by S. Schoenbaum, *Internal Evidence and Elizabethan Dramatic Authorship* (1966), p. 84 (from *Modern Language Review*, XIII, 1918, p. 101).

[10]   The following is a very brief and selective summary of the authorship question. For fuller discussion see Jackson, Wine, and the relevant works cited in Levenson's bibliography (see 'Further Reading').

It is not surprising, however, considering the literary qualities and theatrical skill of the play, that the claims have centred on the three most notable dramatists known to have been working in London in the late 1580s and early 1590s — Marlowe, Kyd, and Shakespeare.

The case for Kyd was first made in 1891 by F. G. Fleay,[11] and later developed by Charles Crawford,[12] who based his ascription on parallels between *Arden* and two works supposed to be by Kyd: the play *Soliman and Perseda* and a pamphlet, *The Murder of John Brewen*.

That Kyd is the author of *Soliman and Perseda* is, at best, doubtful, and the attribution to him of *John Brewen* now completely discredited. The opinion of most recent commentators is summed up in Arthur Freeman's view that arguments in favour of Kyd's authorship of *Arden* are most unconvincing since 'with the removal of *John Brewen* from Kyd's definite canon, many of the natural parallels of expression and subject-matter ... as well, perhaps, as the original suggestion, go entirely by the board.'[13]

The case for Marlowe (seen generally as a collaborator rather than as sole author), was first made by E. H. C. Oliphant in 1926,[14] again on the strength of textual parallels, and subsequently supported by the suggestion of a link between Marlowe's Kentish origins and the large number of local topographical references in the play. As Jackson says (p. 126), however, no 'convincing reasons have been given for ascribing *Arden* to Marlowe.'

The most persistent and intriguing claim is, of course, that made for Shakespeare. As Wine says, the question ' "Did Shakespeare write *Arden of Faversham?*" ... is the only one likely to arouse serious interest', though since M. P. Jackson's detailed analysis in 1963 and Wine's own contributions in his edition (offered 'without at all trying to press for Shakespearean authorship'),[15] there have been no substantial reworkings of the arguments, for or against.

The external evidence to support an ascription to Shakespeare (or anyone else) is non-existent. The play was published in three quarto editions without having a name put to it, Hemminges and Condell

[11]   F.G. Fleay, *Biographical Chronicle*, Vol. II (1891), p. 29.

[12]   C. Crawford, 'The Authorship of *Arden of Feversham*', *Shakespeare-Jahrbuch*, XXXIX (1903), 74–86; reprinted in *Collecteana*, 1st Series (Stratford upon Avon, 1906), pp. 101–30.

[13]   Arthur Freeman, *Thomas Kyd* (1967), pp. 179–80.

[14]   E.H.C. Oliphant, 'Marlowe's Hand in *Arden of Feversham*: a problem for critics', *New Criterion*, IV (1926), 76–93.

[15]   Wine, p. lxxxi and p. lxxxix respectively. Though see R.F. Fleissner, ' "The Secret'st Man of Blood": Foreshadowings of *Macbeth* in *Arden of Faversham*', *University of Dayton Review*, 14, I, 1979–80, 7–13.

did not include it in the First Folio (1623), and it was not among the apocryphal plays added, with *Pericles*, to the second issue of the Third Folio in 1664.

In 1770 a Faversham antiquary, Edward Jacob, published an edition of the play, claiming (on very shaky evidence) that it had good grounds to be considered as Shakespeare's 'earliest theatrical production'. This was thought to be the first attribution to Shakespeare until W. W. Greg noted[16] an entry in a play-catalogue of 1656 ascribing the play to 'Richard Bernard' which, Greg demonstrated, was a compositor's error for Shakespeare's name. Greg points out, however, that the other 'blunders' of Edward Archer, the catalogue's publisher, 'are so many and so gross that very little reliance can be placed on any particular ascription he might make.'

Any ascription must rest, therefore, on internal evidence alone, and although most critics who have turned their attention to the question of authorship are agreed on the play's quality, they are divided on whether that excellence can be identified as specifically and undeniably Shakespeare's. Kenneth Muir, for example, considers *Arden* the 'best of the apocryphal plays', but still argues that it 'does not resemble in style or theme any of Shakespeare's acknowledged plays.'[17]

Other critics, however, have found strong similarities between *Arden* and, particularly, the *Henry VI* trilogy and *Richard III* in their style, language and imagery, and in their presentation of a ruthless and amoral world.[18] To this one might add that the author of *Arden* uses the events of the recent past as set out in Holinshed's *Chronicles* to illuminate and comment on aspects of public life in his own time, just as Shakespeare used such events to provide 'mirrors of Elizabethan policy'.[19]

The most extensive argument in favour of Shakespeare's authorship is presented by M. P. Jackson. He reviews the whole question thoroughly and analyzes the play in great detail, drawing the threads of his argument together in a study of Scene VIII, which he describes as 'lying in every respect beyond the achievement of any known early Elizabethan dramatist except Shakespeare' (p. 250), and he concludes that the evidence provided by this scene and the play as

---

[16] W.W. Greg, 'Shakespeare and *Arden of Feversham*', *Review of English Studies*, XXI (1945), 134–6.

[17] K. Muir, *Shakespeare As Collaborator* (1960), p. 3.

[18] See e.g., M.B. Smith, *Marlowe's Imagery and the Marlowe Canon* (1940); Wine, pp. lxxxix–xci; Jackson.

[19] See Lily B. Campbell, *Shakespeare's Histories* (1947), particularly pp. 72–75.

a whole must give *Arden* 'a fair claim to admittance to the Shakespeare canon.'

While the evidence is still only internal, however, no such firm ascription can be made, especially as the assessment of that evidence is made more than usually difficult by the corrupt nature of the text (see below, p. xxviii).[20]

The undoubted strengths of the play — the complexity of its characterization, the linking of language and themes, the interweaving of public and private issues, and the constant awareness of the potential of the theatrical experience — demonstrate that the author was a master playwright, but one whose identity must remain (at least on present evidence), tantalizingly unknown.

A NOTE ON THE INTRODUCTION TO THE PLAY

Just as *Arden of Faversham* has been called the 'best of the [Shakespeare] apocryphal plays', so it is usually credited with being the 'most famous of all Elizabethan domestic tragedies, and unquestionably the best'.[21] But the effort first to define the genre of 'domestic drama', and then to locate *Arden* within it, may be, in this context, of limited usefulness. For not only have critics differed considerably in their views of the play's aims and effects, but also the criteria used to define the genre have been stretched so wide that it is difficult to establish with any broad measure of agreement which plays should be included in it and which should not.[22]

While I acknowledge, therefore, the influence on *Arden* of various kinds of dramatic and non-dramatic literature, and the fact that in its presentation of ordinary, virtually contemporary, men and women in a clearly-drawn English setting, it offered something different from the usual subject matter and milieu of Elizabethan tragedy, for the purposes of this Introduction I will discuss the play on its own terms.

THE PLAY

At the end of the play, Arden lies dead; eventually murdered in his own parlour, and his body dumped on his own land. From one point of view it is the mutilated corpse of a cuckolded husband, killed at

---

[20]   Jackson points out (p. 157) that the least 'contaminated' parts of *Arden* are those that critics have most often been prepared to concede to Shakespeare, and he argues that if other parts were 'original' they, too, might consequently appear better.

[21]   Adams, p. 101. See also H.S. Davies, *Realism in the Drama* (1933), and Sturgess' Introduction.

[22]   See Peter Ure, 'Marriage and Domestic Drama in Heywood and Ford', *English Studies,* Vol. 32 (1951), 200–216.

the instigation of his wife. From another point of view, however, it is the body of a rapacious landowner, whose death was not only desired, but brought about, by men driven to desperate measures by his avariciousness.

The play operates, therefore, on a number of levels. Firstly, it is an exciting 'thriller' (culminating in what is probably the first piece of detective work on the English stage);[23] secondly, it is a study of complex personalities and relationships; and thirdly, it is an attack on the rampant individualism and covetousness of men like Arden, whose actions threaten not only the stability of their own local community, but, by implication, that of society as a whole.

Throughout the play, the dramatist carefully and consciously matches the obviously immoral actions of Alice and Mosby in the 'private' world of the play against Arden's own less obviously immoral—but equally self-seeking and vicious—actions in the 'public' world, as the dramatist seeks to demonstrate that the links between action and morality cannot be severed in *either* case.

Criticism of *Arden* has tended, however, to concentrate on the characters and their relationships, and on the portrayal of Alice in particular.[24] Clearly, the skill and depth of the characterization is one of the main strengths of this remarkable play, but failure to recognize or acknowledge the significance of Arden's public actions can result in an unbalanced view of a very carefully balanced work, and can obscure the playwright's closely interwoven study of private *and* public morality.

In order to understand the ramifications of Arden's actions, and why the public aspects of Holinshed's story should have attracted the attention of a dramatist writing nearly forty years after the events it recounts had happened, it is necessary to examine those actions in the context first of the real-life Arden's, and then of the playwright's, time.

---

[23]   See Chapman, and J. Hanratty, '*Arden of Feversham*', *The Use of English,* IX (1960), 176 – 80. The 'thriller' aspect of *Arden* is not discussed in this Introduction, but it should not be overlooked. My own experience of the tension and excitement it is possible to create in performance in no way tallies with M.C. Bradbrook's view that the effect of the repeated attempts on Arden's life is to make the audience feel 'positively irritated that [Alice] should not succeed' (*Themes and Conventions of Elizabethan Tragedy,* 2nd ed., Cambridge 1980, p. 40).

[24]   Brooke (p. xv), for example, although he finds her 'vulgarized and degraded' by her 'revolting deceit and coarseness of feeling', calls Alice the 'one character of the first magnitude' in the play; Symonds (op.cit., p. 359) describes her as 'the bourgeois Clytemnestra, the Lady Macbeth of county connections'; and Swinburne (*A Study of Shakespeare,* 1920, pp. 139 – 40), as the 'eldest born of that group to which Lady Macbeth and Dionyza belong by right of weird sisterhood.'

Thomas Arden was murdered in 1551, the fourth year of Edward VI's brief reign. The date is important, for it coincides with a time of great social unrest. The debasement of the coinage; marked increases in the already spiralling trend of rising prices; bad harvests; and widespread enclosure of common land, were all factors that contributed to the discontent that at times during Edward's reign erupted into open rebellion. Although, today, we may be able to distinguish the various causes of the hardship suffered by the agrarian population, it was inevitable that, at the time, directly observable causes should be blamed. Among those singled out as being particularly responsible for the widespread distress were the landlords, and especially those 'new men' who had benefitted from the distribution of land that followed the dissolution of the monasteries, and who looked on that land as the passport to wealth and social status, to gain which they were prepared to break the traditional bonds between landlord and tenant: in other words men like Thomas Arden.[25]

Arden was, in many ways, a typical man of his time, made and raised by the Tudors. Born in Wye (about 12 miles south of Faversham), apparently of a good family, he first made his mark working for Sir Edward North (who had done as well as any out of the Dissolution), in the Court of Augmentations, which had been set up to deal with the revenue and litigation arising from the Crown's disposal of the monastic land. Arden's career progressed well, and marriage to Sir Edward's stepdaughter, Alice Mirfyn, was followed by his appointment to the lucrative post of Controller of the Customs for the port of Faversham. Settled in Kent, Arden soon obtained the land and revenues of the Abbey of Faversham from Sir Thomas Cheiny, who had received the land from Henry VIII in 1540. Once possessed of the property, Arden and his family took up residence in a house by the Abbey wall and he 'continued to amass wealth and to dispossess the other owners of Abbey lands, until he became the foremost citizen in Faversham.'[26]

Inevitably, with nine-tenths of the population living and working directly on the land, criticism of the behaviour of men like Arden was extensive. It was frequently the topic of pamphlets and sermons, and a special 'Prayer for Landlords' was even included in the 1553 *Book of Private Prayer*:

> We heartily pray thee, to send thy holy Spirit into the hearts of them that possess the grounds, pastures, and dwelling places of the earth, that they . . . may not rack and stretch out the rents of their houses and lands . . . after the manner of covetous worldlings.

[25] See Elton, Fletcher, and Hill under 'Further Reading'.

[26] Cust, p. 114.

There is a striking similarity between certain speeches in the play attacking Arden's public actions, and pamphlets attacking the landlords. In one such pamphlet, *An Informacion and Peticion* (1548),[27] the author, Robert Crowley, condemns the landlords' lack of compassion to those dependent on them with the same vehemence as Reede uses in cursing Arden in the play (XIII, 30–8):

> And if any of them perish through your default, know then for certain that the blood of them shall be required at your hands. If the impotent creatures perish for lack of necessaries, you are the murderers, for you have their inheritance and do not minister unto them.

In *The Way to Wealth* (a pamphlet which appeared in the same year as Arden died) the same author indicted men like Arden in terms very similar to Greene's in Scene I (474–7), accusing them of being:

> Men without conscience. Men utterly void of God's fear. Yea, men that live as though there were no God at all! Men that would have all in their own hands; . . .[28]

What has not previously been noted, however, is the *significance* of this particular parallel, for *The Way to Wealth* is not simply an attack on the avariciousness of landlords, but a discussion of the causes and dangers of civil unrest, a constant fear throughout the sixteenth century, and a burning issue in the wake of the uprisings of the late 1540s. Although Crowley naturally condemns sedition, he isolates as one of its main causes the provocation to the poor of the landlords' rack-renting, engrossing, and enclosing for their own profit, the effect of which, he argues, was to drive normally peaceful, God-fearing men to extremes of action, just as, in the play, Arden's actions drive Greene ('A man. . . of great devotion' I, 587) and Reede to take desperate measures.

Although, as E.P. Cheyney writes, the 'greatest distress among the people . . . falls in the short reign of Edward VI',[29] the problems caused by those who put their 'private profit before common gain'[30] were not confined to the middle years of the sixteenth century, and neither was the criticism of their actions.

The closing years of Elizabeth's reign witness the beginning of the retreat of the 'moral economy'.[31] By the middle of the seventeenth century the split had become clearly defined between those who

---

[27] Robert Crowley, *An Informacion and Peticion,* Early English Text Society, Extra Series, No. XV (1872), 151–176.

[28] Robert Crowley, *The Way To Wealth,* p. 132.

[29] E.P. Cheyney, *Social Changes in the Sixteenth Century* (1895), p. 5.

[30] See 'marginal gloss', Appendix, p. 110.

[31] See Joyce Appleby, *Economic Thought and Ideology in Seventeenth Century England* (1978), especially Chapter 3, pp. 52–72.

continued to apply traditional moral censure to economic practice
and those who argued that such strictures were irrelevant since
economic behaviour was determined by necessity rather than human
weakness. But even then, when the 'critical link between action and
responsibility had been cut', specific areas of economic activity
'remained vulnerable to the scrutiny of moralists':[32] the grain trade
(in times of famine); usury; and the enclosure of land. For although
by the time of the play's composition enclosing was past the peak
levels of the mid-century, its effects were well remembered. The
whole question of land ownership and use 'still inspired outspoken
sermons from the pulpit, and stirred passions and community
loyalties in the field',[33] and *moral* condemnation of 'men that would
have all in their own hands' was as sharp as when Crowley wrote his
pamphlet.[34]

The following extract from a poem by Sir Francis Hubert,[35]
written sometime between 1597 and 1600 (after the disastrously wet
summers of the mid-1590s had ruined the harvests, causing the price
of grain to soar), in which he attacks those corn-hoarders who sell at
inflated prices in times of famine, is typical of the criticism of those
covetous for their own wealth:

> But neither fear of God nor love of men,
> Nor common care of public misery,
> Can cause compassionate respect in them;
> For they are branned in their iniquity,
> And must be bridled by authority.

The specific target may be different, but it is a tone and viewpoint
shared by the author of *Arden,* and further indication that, as L.C.
Knights says (quoting, respectively, a letter of 1623 and a
Proclamation of 1598):

> To describe a class of men as 'a kind of people aiming only at their own
> profit' was sufficient to condemn them in the eyes of the right thinking,
> and the Tudor bug-bears — forestallers, regrators, and engrossers — were
> noted for their 'wicked and insatiable greediness' in 'preferring their own
> private gain above the public good'.[36]

The audiences who saw *Arden* performed from the late 1580s
through to the 1630s would, therefore, have perceived the social

---

[32]   Ibid., p. 53.

[33]   Joan Thirsk, 'Enclosing and Engrossing', in Joan Thirsk (ed.), *The Agrarian
History of England and Wales,* Vol. IV 1500–1640, (Cambridge 1967), p. 200.

[34]   In 1597, the government revived the statutes against enclosing and engrossing.

[35]   Quoted in Christopher Hill, *Reformation to Industrial Revolution* (1967), p. 96.
Cf. IV, 1–10.

[36]   L.C. Knights, *Drama and Society in the Age of Jonson* (Penguin edition 1962), p.
126. See also Chapters 1–4.

issues and implications of the play as being directly relevant to their own time, and not as just the historical background to a murder story. They would have recognized in the character of Arden a contemporary type — a social criminal whose 'creed . . . was a doctrineless individualism',[37] and whose actions were a threat to the stability of society.

So while it is true that the play is not merely a 'dramatized sociological tract',[38] to see Arden as a 'good man touched somewhat by avarice',[39] or to suggest that his behaviour as a 'grasping and unscrupulous' landholder is 'not given any emphasis in the play until the strange appearance of Reede',[40] is to fail to grasp that the playwright could expect a knowledge of, and attitude towards, Arden and his actions, without the need to elaborate more than he does.

The points made so far also indicate that the playwright's efforts to establish the sense of a physical environment and of a community where men have 'occupations as well as passions'[41] are the result of his desire to create — within the theatrical means at his disposal — as realistic and tangible a setting as possible for a play in which public actions figure so prominently.

Even more significant is the care with which the social structure within the play is defined. In fact, *Arden* presents what amounts to a microcosm of rural Tudor society. From Lord Cheiny at the apex down to Reede at the bottom, all the characters are clearly placed in the social hierarchy. Even Black Will and Shakebag, far from being merely stock dramatic types, are representative of 'that dread of sixteenth-century society — the masterless man',[42] who haunted the streets of London and the road to the coast.

Perhaps Franklin provides the best example of the dramatist's concern to locate each character's social status as precisely as possible. The playwright's own invention, Franklin's main function in the play is to provide someone to whom Arden can confess his inmost thoughts without the constant need for soliloquy, and to act as a spokesman on the otherwise isolated Arden's behalf. Beyond this, the character remains largely undeveloped as an individual personality. His social status is made quite clear, however, not only by implication as Arden's friend, but also by the obvious significance

---

[37]   Thomas Wilson, *A Discourse Upon Usury*, 1572 (edited, with an Introduction, by R.H. Tawney, 1925), Intro., p. 170.

[38]   Wine, p. lxiv.

[39]   Bluestone, p. 175.

[40]   Madeline Doran, *Endeavors of Art* (Madison, 1954), p. 351.

[41]   Philip Edwards, *Thomas Kyd and Early Elizabethan Tragedy* (1966), p. 20.

[42]   Chapman, p. 16.

The county of Kent, from John Speed's The Theatre of the Empire of Great Britain, *1611.*

of his name[43] and by the reference to his 'house in Aldersgate Street',[44] which at the time of the play's composition was one of the most fashionable addresses in London — a fact that would certainly not go unnoticed by the original audience.

With certain characters — Lord Cheiny and Dick Reede, for example — the playwright deliberately indicates no more than their position in the social hierarchy, since in each case it is this rather than any individual qualities that is of greatest importance.[45] It should be realized, however, that if the world these characters inhabit is clearly defined in terms of its social structure — through, for example, close attention to costume, speech and social behaviour, class attitudes — this method of presentation will make them no less effective dramatically than those characters who are more fully drawn.[46]

The 'private' world of the play is centred around the personalities and relationships of the three main characters, the struggle between them and — more strikingly — within themselves, as the playwright explores with remarkable psychological depth their 'disturbed thoughts' and inner conflicts.

Arden alone of the three main protagonists inhabits both the 'public' and 'private' worlds of the play. His is the central, pivotal role, and to sustain it the playwright has created possibly his most complex character. He is torn between his avowedly deep love for Alice (I, 39), and his loathing for her adultery, a reaction made the more acute by the fact that her lover is of such inferior social status in his eyes ('A botcher, and no better at the first'), and because the affair has become the 'common table-talk' of 'all the knights and gentlemen of Kent' (I, 343–4). It is this mixture of conflicting attitudes in Arden that accounts for the contradictory nature of much of his behaviour. Although, for example, an audience might find his sudden capitulation to Alice in Scene XIII (11. 117–21 and

[43] A Franklin was one who owned a certain amount of land freehold.

[44] See II, 99 and n.

[45] See Arnold Hauser, 'The Origins of Domestic Drama', in E. Bentley (ed.), *The Theory of the Modern Stage* (1968), pp. 403–419. Hauser's essay is mainly concerned with later drama and makes no specific reference to *Arden*, but many of the points he makes are pertinent and illuminating.

[46] Barry Kyle's production of Rowley, Dekker and Ford's *The Witch of Edmonton* for the Royal Shakespeare Company, which opened at The Other Place in Stratford upon Avon in September 1981, demonstrated how such an approach might be successfully employed. The social detail in the setting and performances brought, as Irving Wardle wrote in his review (*The Times*, 18 September 1981), 'the dark side of rural England . . . fully into view.'

130 – 51) bewildering or foolish, even derisory, if the contradictions
within him (revealed in I, 33 – 43, for example) are established from
the beginning, and if each attitude is played with equal conviction,
the audience will come to recognize that the 'devil' that drives Arden
(XIII, 152) is his own confused mind, and that the contradictions in
his behaviour are a result of this, not of the dramatist's failure to
present a consistent characterization.

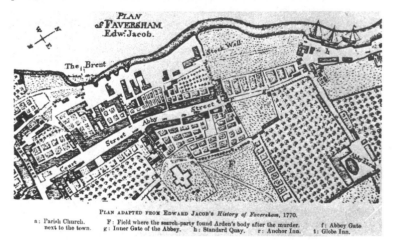

Plan of Faversham. 'f' indicates the site of Arden's house.
(Reproduced from Cust, p. 105)

The changes made by the playwright in his source material
indicate (as with other main characters) his desire to avoid a one-
sided, one-dimensional portrayal of Arden, but despite these
changes, and the other points that might be advanced in Arden's
favour (eg. Franklin's friendship, Cheiny's respect, Michael's
acknowledgement of his kindness), his public actions weigh heavily
against him. The playwright highlights them by, for example, the
telling juxtaposition of Arden's apparent willingness to see Reede's
family starve (XIII, 19 – 27), with his and Franklin's smugly satisfied
appraisal of the 'most bounteous and liberal' (XIII, 68) hospitality
they themselves have just enjoyed, and it is hard to find in this
fascinatingly complex — but still unattractive — character the 'best
instincts for affection, generosity and trust' of which Wine writes,[47]
especially in his dealings with those who need the benefit of such
instincts most.

[47]   Wine, p. lxx.

Alice and Mosby, too, are driven by passions that overcome their rational judgments. For Alice it is her irresistible sexual passion for Mosby, while he is motivated by the more mundane, though no less compelling, desire for the wealth and social status that his relationship with Alice promises to provide. Even when he recognizes the price he must pay to achieve his ambition (VIII, 1–18), he cannot relinquish it, 'But needs must on although to danger's gate' (VIII, 22); and when Alice's well-aimed insults impel him to leave he is won round not by her references to their love, nor even by her desperate and blasphemous act of tearing her prayerbook, but by her flattery ('Sweet Mosby is as gentle as a king', VIII, 140), the true nature of which he recognizes ('Ah, how you women can insinuate' VIII, 146), but which he cannot resist. It is revealing that whereas Alice kills her husband for 'hindering Mosby's love and mine', Mosby kills Arden in revenge for 'the pressing iron you told me of'. In Carrère's apt phrase, 'this calculating spirit is at the mercy of a fearful body',[48] and in a play of sharp ironies one of the most fitting is that what finally proves Mosby's guilt is the purse he stole from his victim.[49]

In Holinshed, Alice evinces no remorse whatsoever until she makes a sudden volte-face at the end. In the play, however, far from being 'unaffected by any sense of wrongdoing'[50] her rapid shifts of thought and action are clear signs of a mind under pressure. She fluctuates between seeing Mosby as her 'Endymion' and as a 'base peasant', and although she is for the most part determined that Arden should die (even at the last moment taking the dagger and stabbing him herself), the moments in the play (I, 194–204 and 213–16; VIII, 63–79 and 106–109; XIV, 261), when she recognizes the reality of the situation, or seems close to repenting, need to be strongly pointed. They prepare the way for her behaviour at the end of the play and make clear that when, confronted with the accusing symbol of the bleeding body, she first confesses and then repents, it is not a shift from realistic to conventional behaviour, but a progression from, and mixture of, her behaviour throughout the play.

---

[48]   F. Carrère (ed.), *Arden de Faversham* (1950), p. 76 ('. . . cet esprit calculateur est à la merci d'un corps peureux, . . .').

[49]   This detail is the playwright's invention. According to Holinshed (see Appendix, p. 107), the incriminating evidence was the blood spattered on Mosby's own purse.

[50]   Philip Edwards, op.cit., p. 21.

The repentance, brief in itself (XVI, 7–11 and XVIII, 9–11), comes only after a last desperate attempt to brazen it out has failed (XIV, 408–10: Franklin, unlike his murdered friend is not at all confused in his attitude to Alice); she refuses to accept direct responsibility for her actions, blaming Mosby's 'villainies' and the frailties of youth (XVIII, 14–18); and she ignores more or less entirely the despairing plea for help from the innocent — but condemned — Bradshaw.

In the final scene of Thomas Heywood's *A Woman Killed With Kindness* (1603), which is similar to *Arden* in a number of ways, the audience can respond to Anne's and Frankford's sincere and intense expression of repentance and forgiveness, and the pervading mood is one of reconciliation. *Arden*, however, culminates (XVIII, 33–8) in what Bluestone describes as 'a litany of repentance, hatred, despair, hope, a near-jest, and a curse.'[51] It is a mixture of emotions characteristic of the play as a whole, and an ending to which we can only respond uneasily, aware that anything but real justice has been done.

As I have tried to show, the social comment constitutes the 'public' world of the play (with the central motif of *land*), and the exploration of the personalities and relationships of Arden, Alice, and Mosby constitutes the 'private', although in practice, of course, the play is less schematized, the issues less separable, than my analysis may suggest. The playwright is concerned to show that in both public and private life — though their objectives may be different — men and women are driven to commit immoral acts by similar covetous urges, and the structure of the play is designed to establish the affinity between *all* these actions.[52]

Arden, then, presents a picture of a society where the values of life, and even life itself, have become commodities to be bought and sold. Arden himself draws the threads together when he says:

As for the lands, Mosby, they are mine
By letters patents from his majesty.
But I must have a mandate for my wife;
They say you seek to rob me of her love.   (I, 300–4)

Mosby does seek to rob Arden of Alice, just as Arden seeks to 'rob' others of their land; Mosby's sister, Susan, is his to 'grant' to another, just as Arden 'hath the grant' of all the Abbey lands; Michael fears to be 'rifled' of his purse, while Alice claims she has been 'rifled' of her honour; and Mosby sees his unprofitable relationship with Alice as 'wrapping' his 'credit' in her 'company'.

---

[51]   Bluestone, p. 182. See Glynne Wickham, *Shakespeare's Dramatic Heritage* (1969), p. 56, for a different interpretation.

[52]   Cf. Wine, p. lxiv.

The overall world of the play is one of immoral acts, where men and women scorn to keep their oaths and twist morality to their own ends. Alice dismisses her marriage vows as merely 'words, and words is wind,/And wind is mutable' (I, 436–7), while Arden clings tenaciously to his legal right to Reede's land (XIII, 19–20), in the face of a clear moral obligation to relent.

This sense of a world of distorted values is sharpened by the skilful use of comedy in the play, most notably in the actions of Black Will and Shakebag, which are set in increasingly stark contrast to the reality of the situation, but there is grim humour, too, in an exchange such as:

ALICE
    Yet nothing could enforce me to the deed
    But Mosby's love. Might I without control
    Enjoy thee still, then Arden should not die;
    But seeing I cannot, therefore let him die.
MOSBY
    Enough, sweet Alice, thy kind words makes me melt.

                                                    (I, 173–7)

where Mosby's response is genuinely grotesque in that it simultaneously provokes laughter — however uneasy — and disgust.[53]

The depiction of a savage and ruthless world, a world in chaos, is reinforced by the play's language and imagery.[54] The verbal imagery is predominantly of animals; hunting and snaring; inversions of religion; of darkness subsuming the light; the dismemberment of the human body; and, significantly, of the unweeded land, a common Renaissance figure for disorder in the state, but also used in *Arden* to link still more tightly the parallels between family (or private) and social disorder (see, for example, IV, 1–13; VIII, passim).[55]

The visual imagery, too, is based mainly on inversion: the food intended to poison; the crucifix intended to kill; the prayer-book destroyed to provide a repository for adulterous love letters.

The playwright also creates a number of striking stage images which enforce many of the play's ideas: the Ferryman in the mist, with echoes of Charon conveying the damned to Hell; the toast that conceals a pledge to murder (XIV, 205–220); Arden (having survived in the savage outside world seemingly by the constant intervention of Chance), literally rolling dice for his life in the

---

[53]   See also, e.g., XIV, 205–212.

[54]   See the detailed studies of the play's language and imagery in Bluestone, Ousby, and Youngblood.

[55]   See above, pp. xx–xxii.

'safety' of his own parlour; the body of the avaricious man laid in his countinghouse.

This pervading sense of chaos is measured against an increasing awareness of wider forces at work. Throughout the play characters recognize — either directly or obliquely — the wrong they do in their lives, and yet, divided within themselves they ignore (or are blind to), the very signs that might save them. The events of Scene XIII offer first Arden (11. 1–76), and then Alice and her fellow conspirators (11. 77–155), what proves to be their last opportunity to relent. Once this is rejected, the acts of Chance, or Providence, that throughout might have warned both Arden and his killers, are responsible first for trapping the victim (the rolling of the dice) and his murderers (the blood cleaving to the ground, the snow suddenly stopping), and then for demonstrating the mutual guilt of Arden and Alice.

Frontispiece to the 1633 Quarto, illustrating the murder of Arden.

The opening lines of the play established the driving forces behind Arden and Alice — his desire for land and status, hers for Mosby. At the close of the play, the action of placing Arden's lacerated body on the Abbey land forms a powerful image which literally embodies the disruption and dislocation of family and society brought about as the result of Arden's and Alice's lives lived without regard for others, and in the relentless pursuit of their own aims.[56]

[56]   Cf. Youngblood, p. 218. See also Peter M. Daly, *Literature in the Light of the Emblem* (Toronto, 1979), who writes (p. 147) that in the tragedy of the period '. . . the corpse is not simply a dead character, but a warning to others to learn certain truths from his death; the corpse is an emblem that instructs.'

Alice recognizes for herself the meaning of the still-bleeding body:

> The more I sound his name the more he bleeds.
> This blood condemns me, . . .   (XVI, 4–5)

But Arden has been an aggressor as well as a victim, and it is Franklin (his words lent greater weight by the role he has played as Arden's only friend), who, at the very end of the play, emphasizes the wider implications of the image:

> But this above the rest is to be noted:
> Arden lay murdered in that plot of ground
> Which he by force and violence held from Reede;
> And in the grass his body's print was seen
> Two years and more after the deed was done.
>   (Epilogue, 9–13)

NOTE ON THE TEXT

THE FIRST QUARTO of *Arden of Faversham* was published in 1592, and second and third quartos followed in 1599 and 1633. Comparison shows that Q3 was printed from Q2, and Q2 from Q1, which establishes Q1 as the basic copy for any edition. Detailed collation of the three extant copies of Q1 reveals only minor press variants.

Opinion on the nature of the text of Q1 is divided between those who see it as a 'remarkably good'[57] text displaying 'general coherence',[58] and those who consider it a 'bad' quarto: that is, a published text derived from the memory of an actor (or actors) and reported to a scribe, or from transcripts of the actors' roles, or from a combination of these methods.[59]

The text shows many signs of such means of construction — frequent repetitions of words, tags, phrases, even of whole lines; parallels with other plays; poor versification; unnecessary retelling of incidents already seen by the audience; and inconsistencies in the plot.

On the other hand, the text has obviously been carefully prepared for the printer with, on the whole, well-placed and informative stage directions. The text was set by one compositor, who had the habit of setting prose as verse.

[57]   Brooke, p. xiii.

[58]   *Arden of Feversham*, Scolar Press 1972, 'Note'.

[59]   See Jackson, Wine, and Alfred Hart, *Stolne and Surreptitious Copies* (1942).

Three copies of Q1 survive (the Malone, at the Bodleian Library; the Dyce, at the Victoria and Albert Museum; and the Mostyn-Perry at the Huntington Library), three of Q2 (one at the Folger Shakespeare Library and two at the Huntington Library), and numerous copies of Q3.

This edition is based on the Scolar Press facsimile of the Malone copy of Q1 in the Bodleian Library: shelf-mark MAL 208 (3). I have also consulted a microfilm of the Folger Library's copy of Q2, and the Bodleian Library's copy of Q3: shelf-mark MAL 163 (1). M. L. Wine consulted all extant copies of Q1 and Q2 and 19 copies of Q3 in preparing his Revels edition and I have, therefore, paid great attention to it.

The corrupt state of much of the text leads Jackson (p. 36) to argue for 'less conservative editing' than the play has received in the past for, he concludes, 'it is safe to emend the *Arden* Quarto rather freely on metrical grounds, at least when the elimination of an easily identifiable actor's tag seems called for' (p. 47). This edition, however, takes Fredson Bowers' view (quoted by Jackson, p. 40) that '. . . we can often be aware of corruption in the "bad" text (though not always), but we may have no concrete evidence at all about the autograph reading which has been memorially corrupted. To attempt, therefore, to reconstruct a purely hypothetical text by metrical smoothing and verbal emendation is sheer folly except in isolated special cases.'[60]

There is, however, a wide measure of agreement among editors on the need to reset much of Q1's verse as prose. I have followed Wine in this, and in his lineation (except at IX, 55–6), but have not recorded these changes from Q1 in the notes.

Again in common with other editors I have re-punctuated the text, as Q1's punctuation is indiscriminate and non-authorial, but I have drawn attention to it in the notes only where alternative punctuation would affect the meaning. Spelling has been modernized throughout.

Stage directions (which usually indicate the moment when a movement is initiated on stage)[61] have generally been left where they stand in the text, but I have inserted further directions (in square brackets) where they may clarify stage action. The 'aside' has been indicated (again, in square brackets), where it is not immediately apparent from the text. Speech headings have been expanded.

---

[60]   See Fredson Bowers, *The Dramatic Works of Thomas Dekker*, I (1953), pp. 399–404.

[61]   Though they do not anticipate the move sufficiently to suggest a prompt-copy. See Jackson, pp. 5–10.

Following the practice of this series, only substantive emendations to the copy-text have been recorded. The abbreviation 'ed.' means any editor at any time. *Arden* contains a number of celebrated cruxes, however, and these, as well as a small number of other emendations, have been discussed more fully in the notes.

Finally, I have followed the practice of other recent editors in dividing the play into eighteen scenes and an epilogue.

As well as Wine's edition, I have referred, in particular, to the following modern editions, and the use of the editor's surname in the notes indicates this edition unless otherwise stated: *Arden of Feversham, a Tragedy*, ed. A.H. Bullen (1887); *Arden of Feversham*, ed. R. Bayne (1897); *The Shakespeare Apocrypha*, ed. C. F. Tucker Brooke (1908); *Three Elizabethan Domestic Tragedies*, ed. K. Sturgess (1969).

This edition adopts the modern spelling 'Faversham' throughout.

FURTHER READING

An excellent source of earlier material on Arden is provided by Jill Levenson's bibliography in T. P. Logan and D. S. Smith (eds.), *The Predecessors of Shakespeare: a survey and bibliography of recent studies in English Renaissance Drama*, Nebraska, 1973, which cites major critical studies of the play as well as a comprehensive list of other works.

In addition to the works cited in the footnotes to this edition, the following may be useful in pursuing some of the ideas in the Introduction and Notes:

David Attwell, 'Property, Status, and the Subject in a Middle-Class Tragedy', *English Literary Renaissance*, 21, 1991, 328–48.

Catherine Belsey, 'Alice Arden's Crime' in *The Subject of Tragedy: Identity and Difference in Renaissance Drama*, 1985, pp. 129–48.

Andrew Clark, *Domestic Drama*, Institüt für englische Sprache und Literatur, Universität Salzburg, 1975.

Viviana Comensoli, *Household Business: Domestic Plays of Early Modern England*, Toronto: University of Toronto Press, 1996.

Frances Dolan, 'Home-Rebels and House-Traitors: Murderous Wives in Early Modern England', *Yale Journal of Law and the Humanities*, 4 (1992), 1-31.

Frances E. Dolan, 'The Subject('s) Role: Petty Treason and the Forms of Domestic Rebellion', *Shakespeare Quarterly*, 43, 1992, 317–40.

G.R. Elton, *England Under The Tudors*, 1955.

Anthony Fletcher, *Tudor Rebellions*, 1968.

Christopher Hill, *Reformation to Industrial Revolution*, 1967.

Jonathan Hope, *The Authorship of Shakespeare's Plays: A Socio-Linguistic Study*, Cambridge: Cambridge University Press, 1994 (especially pages 128–131).

Patricia Hyde, *Thomas Arden in Faversham: The Man Behind the Myth*, Faversham: Faversham Society, 1996.

Alexander Leggatt, *'Arden of Faversham'*, *Shakespeare Survey*, 36, 1983, 121–133.

Leonore Lieblein, 'The Context of Murder in English Domestic Plays, 1590-1610', *Studies in English Literature*, 23, 1983, 181–96.

Lena Cowen Orlin, *Private Matter and Public Culture in Post-Reformation England,* Ithaca and London: Cornell University Press, 1994.

Julie R. Schutzman, 'Alice Arden's Freedom and the Suspended Moment in *'Arden of Faversham'*, *Studies in English Literature,* 36, 1996, 289-314.

Garrett A. Sullivan, Jr, '"Arden lay murdered in that plot of ground": surveying, land and *Arden of Faversham',* *English Literary History,* 61, No. 2, Summer 1994, 231–52.

E.P. Walz, *'Arden of Faversham* as Tragic Satire', *Massachusetts Studies in English,* 4, II, 1973, 23–41.

Frank Whigham, *Seizures of the Will in Early Modern English Drama,* Cambridge: Cambridge University Press, 1996.

Helen C White, *Social Criticism in Popular Religious Literature of the Sixteenth Century,* New York, 1944.

Keith Wrightson, *English Society 1580-1680,* 1982.

THE
LAMENTA:
BLE AND TRVE TRA-
GEDIE OF M. AR-
DEN OF FEVERSHAM
IN KENT.

Who was moſt wickedlye murdered, by
the meanes of his diſloyall and wanton
wyfe, who for the loue ſhe bare to one
Moſbie, hyred two deſperat ruf-
fins Blackwill and Shakbag,
to kill him.

Wherin is ſhewed the great mal-
lice and diſcimulation of a wicked woman, the vnſatiable deſire of filthie luſt
and the ſhamefull end of all
murderers.

Imprinted at London for Edward
White, dwelling at the lyttle North
dore of Paules Church at
the ſigne of the
Gun. 1592.
✽

[Dramatis Personae
in order of appearance

ARDEN
FRANKLIN, *his friend*
ALICE, *Arden's wife*
ADAM FOWLE, *landlord of the Flower-de-Luce*
MICHAEL, *Arden's servant*
MOSBY
CLARKE, *a painter*
GREENE
SUSAN, *Mosby's sister and Alice's servingmaid*
BRADSHAW, *a goldsmith*
BLACK WILL ⎫
SHAKEBAG ⎬ *hired murderers*
A PRENTICE ⎭
LORD CHEINY, *and his* MEN
A FERRYMAN
DICK REEDE
A SAILOR, *his friend*
MAYOR OF FAVERSHAM, *and the* WATCH]

THE TRAGEDY OF
MASTER ARDEN OF FAVERSHAM

Scene I

Enter ARDEN *and* FRANKLIN

FRANKLIN
  Arden, cheer up thy spirits and droop no more.
  My gracious Lord the Duke of Somerset
  Hath freely given to thee and to thy heirs,
  By letters patents from his majesty,
  All the lands of the Abbey of Faversham.   5
  Here are the deeds,
  Sealed and subscribed with his name and the king's.
  Read them, and leave this melancholy mood.
ARDEN
  Franklin, thy love prolongs my weary life;
  And, but for thee, how odious were this life,   10
  That shows me nothing but torments my soul,
  And those foul objects that offend mine eyes;
  Which makes me wish that for this veil of heaven
  The earth hung over my head and covered me.
  Love letters pass 'twixt Mosby and my wife,   15
  And they have privy meetings in the town.
  Nay, on his finger did I spy the ring
  Which at our marriage day the priest put on.
  Can any grief be half so great as this?
FRANKLIN
  Comfort thyself, sweet friend; it is not strange   20
  That women will be false and wavering.
ARDEN
  Ay, but to dote on such a one as he
  Is monstrous, Franklin, and intolerable.

---

11 *shows* affords
13 *for this veil of heaven* instead of the sky
15 *pass* ed. (past Qq)

---

2 *Duke of Somerset* Edward Seymour, the Duke of Somerset, (born c. 1506) was
  appointed Lord Protector in 1547, on the accession of Edward VI (*his majesty*, 1.
  4), at the age of nine. Somerset was executed in 1552.
4 *letters patents* Open letters or documents, usually from a sovereign, conferring
  some right, title, property or office.

FRANKLIN
  Why, what is he?
ARDEN
  A botcher, and no better at the first,   25
  Who, by base brokage getting some small stock,
  Crept into service of a nobleman,
  And by his servile flattery and fawning
  Is now become the steward of his house,
  And bravely jets it in his silken gown.   30
FRANKLIN
  No nobleman will count'nance such a peasant.
ARDEN
  Yes, the Lord Clifford, he that loves not me.
  But through his favour let not him grow proud,
  For were he by the Lord Protector backed,
  He should not make me to be pointed at.   35
  I am by birth a gentleman of blood,
  And that injurious ribald that attempts
  To violate my dear wife's chastity—
  For dear I hold her love, as dear as heaven—

25 *at the first* in his origins (Sturgess)
26 *base brokage* 1. pimping (see I.604–7) 2. shady business deals
30 *bravely jets it* ostentatiously swaggers about
37 *injurious* insulting, slanderous
   ribald Q3 (riball Q1–2) 1. base fellow 2. lewd, wanton

---

25 *botcher* 'A mender of old clothes; the same to a tailor as a cobbler to a shoemaker' (Johnson).
29 *steward* The official who controlled the domestic arrangements of a large household, and, therefore, a position of importance and responsibility.
30 *silken gown* A gown, chain, and white staff were the insignia of a steward's office.
32 *Lord Clifford* In fact, according to Holinshed, Mosby was the servant of Sir Edward (later Lord) North, Alice's step-father and Arden's former master (see Intro., p. xix). No mention is made of these facts in the play, however, and the fictional 'Lord Clifford' is substituted. Cust (p. 114) suggests that the alteration was 'probably made to prevent scandal in the North family.' Sir Thomas North, Alice's step-brother and the translator of Plutarch, was still alive when the play was printed.
33 *his* i.e. Lord Clifford's *him* i.e. Mosby
36 *gentleman of blood* 'One who is entitled to bear arms, though not ranking among the nobility' (*O.E.D.*). See I, 310–11, and Intro., p. xix.

Shall on the bed which he thinks to defile   40
See his dissevered joints and sinews torn,
Whilst on the planchers pants his weary body,
Smeared in the channels of his lustful blood.

FRANKLIN

Be patient, gentle friend, and learn of me
To ease thy grief and save her chastity.   45
Entreat her fair; sweet words are fittest engines
To raze the flint walls of a woman's breast.
In any case be not too jealous,
Nor make no question of her love to thee;
But, as securely, presently take horse,   50
And lie with me at London all this term;
For women when they may will not,
But being kept back, straight grow outrageous.

ARDEN

Though this abhors from reason, yet I'll try it,
And call her forth, and presently take leave.   55
How, Alice!

Here enters ALICE

ALICE

Husband, what mean you to get up so early?
Summer nights are short, and yet you rise ere day.
Had I been wake you had not risen so soon.

ARDEN

Sweet love, thou know'st that we two, Ovid-like,   60
Have often chid the morning when it 'gan to peep,
And often wished that dark Night's purblind steeds
Would pull her by the purple mantle back
And cast her in the ocean to her love.

42 *planchers* floor boards
46 *entreat her fair* speak gently to her
   engines ie. of war, but also devices, plots
47 *raze* ed. (race Qq)
50 *as securely* as if without misgivings, confidently
   presently immediately
51 *lie* lodge
54 *abhors from* is inconsistent with, repugnant to
59 *risen* ed. (rise Qq)
62 *purblind* totally blind

51 *term* One of the three (or four) sessions of the law courts into which the year was divided.
60-4 *Ovid-like* Compare these lines with Ovid's Elegy XIII in Book I of the *Amores*, translated by Christopher Marlowe.

But this night, sweet Alice, thou hast killed my heart;   65
I heard thee call on Mosby in thy sleep.

ALICE

'Tis like I was asleep when I named him,
For being awake he comes not in my thoughts.

ARDEN

Ay, but you started up and suddenly,
Instead of him, caught me about the neck.   70

ALICE

Instead of him? Why, who was there but you?
And where but one is how can I mistake?

FRANKLIN

Arden, leave to urge her over-far.

ARDEN

Nay, love, there is no credit in a dream.
Let it suffice I know thou lovest me well.   75

ALICE

Now I remember whereupon it came:
Had we no talk of Mosby yesternight?

FRANKLIN

Mistress Alice, I heard you name him once or twice.

ALICE

And thereof came it, and therefore blame not me.

ARDEN

I know it did, and therefore let it pass.   80
I must to London, sweet Alice, presently.

ALICE

But tell me, do you mean to stay there long?

ARDEN

No longer than till my affairs be done.

FRANKLIN

He will not stay above a month at most.

ALICE

A month? Ay me! Sweet Arden, come again   85
Within a day or two or else I die.

---

73 *leave* cease

---

74 Cf. the proverb, 'Dreams are lies' (Tilley, D587).
83 *than* ed. (there Qq). Wine quotes M.P. Jackson (*Notes and Queries*, CCVIII,
   1963 , p. 410), who argues for the emendation on the grounds that ' "then",
   which is the normal Elizabethan spelling of "than", could easily have been
   misread as "there", particularly under the influence of "there" in the previous
   line.'

ARDEN
    I cannot long be from thee, gentle Alice.
    Whilst Michael fetch our horses from the field,
    Franklin and I will down unto the quay,
    For I have certain goods there to unload.   90
    Meanwhile prepare our breakfast, gentle Alice,
    For yet ere noon we'll take horse and away.
                     Exeunt ARDEN *and* FRANKLIN

ALICE
    Ere noon he means to take horse and away!
    Sweet news is this. Oh, that some airy spirit
    Would, in the shape and likeness of a horse,   95
    Gallop with Arden 'cross the ocean
    And throw him from his back into the waves!
    Sweet Mosby is the man that hath my heart,
    And he usurps it, having nought but this—
    That I am tied to him by marriage.   100
    Love is a god, and marriage is but words,
    And therefore Mosby's title is the best.
    Tush! Whether it be or no, he shall be mine
    In spite of him, of Hymen, and of rites.

        Here enters ADAM *of the Flower-de-Luce*

    And here comes Adam of the Flower-de-Luce.   105
    I hope he brings me tidings of my love.
    How now, Adam, what is the news with you?
    Be not afraid, my husband is now from home.

ADAM
    He whom you wot of, Mosby, Mistress Alice,
    Is come to town, and sends you word by me   110
    In any case you may not visit him.

ALICE
    Not visit him?

ADAM
    No, nor take no knowledge of his being here.

---

109 *wot* know

---

  99 *he* i.e. Arden
104 *Hymen* god of marriage
104 s.d. *Flower-de-Luce* An inn, situated in Preston Street, a few minutes walk from
    Arden's house in Abbey Street. The building still stands, but is no longer used
    as a public house. It was purchased by the Faversham Society in 1972, and now
    houses the Fleur de Lis Heritage Centre. ('The prevailing form [*fleur de lis*] . . .
    is scarcely found in Eng. before the 19th c.' *O.E.D.*)

ALICE

But tell me, is he angry or displeased?

ADAM

Should seem so, for he is wondrous sad.   115

ALICE

Were he as mad as raving Hercules
I'll see him. Ay, and were thy house of force,
These hands of mine should raze it to the ground
Unless that thou wouldst bring me to my love.

ADAM

Nay, and you be so impatient, I'll be gone.   120

ALICE

Stay, Adam, stay; thou wert wont to be my friend.
Ask Mosby how I have incurred his wrath;
Bear him from me these pair of silver dice
With which we played for kisses many a time,
And when I lost I won, and so did he—   125
Such winning and such losing Jove send me!
And bid him, if his love do not decline,
To come this morning but along my door,
And as a stranger but salute me there.
This may he do without suspect or fear.   130

ADAM

I'll tell him what you say, and so farewell.

Exit ADAM

ALICE

Do, and one day I'll make amends for all.
I know he loves me well but dares not come
Because my husband is so jealous,
And these my narrow-prying neighbours blab,   135

---

117 *of force* fortified   128 *To come* Q2–3 (Come Q1)
118 *raze* Q3 (race Q1–2)   135 *narrow-prying* Q2–3 (marrow-prying Q1)
120 *and if*

---

116   Hercules was sent a shirt by his wife, Deianira, which she had woven and then
      soaked in the blood of the centaur, Nessus (whom Hercules had killed),
      believing that it would work as a charm to restore her unfaithful husband's love
      to her. In fact, the blood was poisoned, and as soon as Hercules put on the shirt
      he was driven raving mad by the pain and killed himself.

135   As Wine notes, Q1's 'marrow-prying' is striking metaphorically and may be the
      correct reading. A similar expression is used in *Soliman and Perseda*, V.ii, 14
      ('Such is the force of marrow burning loue') and in *Venus and Adonis*, 1. 741
      ('the marrow-eating sickness'), though in both those cases it clearly refers to the
      contemporary belief that the marrow of the bones is a sexual provocative. Q2's
      reading compares with *The Taming of the Shrew*, III.ii, 142 ('The narrow-prying
      father, Minola').

Hinder our meetings when we would confer.
But, if I live, that block shall be removed,
And Mosby, thou that comes to me by stealth,
Shalt neither fear the biting speech of men
Nor Arden's looks. As surely shall he die   140
As I abhor him and love only thee.
             Here enters MICHAEL
How now, Michael, whither are you going?
MICHAEL
To fetch my master's nag. I hope you'll think on me.
ALICE
Ay, but Michael, see you keep your oath,
And be as secret as you are resolute.   145
MICHAEL
I'll see he shall not live above a week.
ALICE
On that condition, Michael, here is my hand:
None shall have Mosby's sister but thyself.
MICHAEL
I understand the painter here hard by
Hath made report that he and Sue is sure.   150
ALICE
There's no such matter, Michael; believe it not.
MICHAEL
But he hath sent a dagger sticking in a heart,
With a verse or two stolen from a painted cloth,
The which I hear the wench keeps in her chest.
Well, let her keep it! I shall find a fellow   155
That can both write and read and make rhyme too,
And if I do—well, I say no more.
I'll send from London such a taunting letter
As she shall eat the heart he sent with salt,
And fling the dagger at the painter's head.   160

137 *block* 1. obstruction 2. hard-hearted person
149 *hard by* near by
150 *sure* betrothed
159 *As* that
     she ed. (not in Qq)

---

153 *painted cloth* as opposed to woven cloth, and therefore a cheap substitute for
tapestry. The design frequently incorporated verses and mottoes. (See Glynne
Wickham, *Early English Stages,* Volume Two 1576 to 1660, Part I, 1963, p. 317,
for their use as draperies in the playhouses.)

ALICE
What needs all this? I say that Susan's thine.

MICHAEL
Why then, I say that I will kill my master,
Or anything that you will have me do.

ALICE
But, Michael, see you do it cunningly.

MICHAEL
Why, say I should be took, I'll ne'er confess   165
That you know anything; and Susan, being a maid,
May beg me from the gallows of the shrieve.

ALICE
Trust not to that, Michael.

MICHAEL
You cannot tell me, I have seen it, I.
But, mistress, tell her whether I live or die   170
I'll make her more worth than twenty painters can,
For I will rid mine elder brother away,
And then the farm of Bolton is mine own.
Who would not venture upon house and land,
When he may have it for a right-down blow?   175

Here enters MOSBY

ALICE
Yonder comes Mosby. Michael, get thee gone,
And let not him nor any know thy drifts.   *Exit* MICHAEL
Mosby, my love!

MOSBY
Away, I say, and talk not to me now.

ALICE
A word or two, sweetheart, and then I will.   180
'Tis yet but early days; thou needest not fear.

MOSBY
Where is your husband?

167 *shrieve* sheriff
171 *worth* wealthy
172 *rid . . . away* i.e. kill
175 *right-down* downright
177 *drifts* schemes, plots
181 *early days* early in the day

166–7 It was a common belief that a virgin could save a man from being hanged by
    offering to marry him.
173 *Bolton* probably Boughton-under-Blean, a village in Kent, a few miles west of
    Canterbury (see map).

ALICE
  'Tis now high water, and he is at the quay.
MOSBY
  There let him be; henceforward know me not.
ALICE
  Is this the end of all thy solemn oaths?   185
  Is this the fruit thy reconcilement buds?
  Have I for this given thee so many favours,
  Incurred my husband's hate, and—out, alas!—
  Made shipwreck of mine honour for thy sake?
  And dost thou say 'henceforward know me not'?   190
  Remember when I locked thee in my closet,
  What were thy words and mine? Did we not both
  Decree to murder Arden in the night?
  The heavens can witness, and the world can tell,
  Before I saw that falsehood look of thine,   195
  'Fore I was tangled with thy 'ticing speech,
  Arden to me was dearer than my soul—
  And shall be still. Base peasant, get thee gone,
  And boast not of thy conquest over me,
  Gotten by witchcraft and mere sorcery.   200
  For what hast thou to countenance my love,
  Being descended of a noble house,
  And matched already with a gentleman
  Whose servant thou may'st be? And so farewell.
MOSBY
  Ungentle and unkind, Alice; now I see   205
  That which I ever feared and find too true:
  A woman's love is as the lightning flame
  Which even in bursting forth consumes itself.
  To try thy constancy have I been strange.
  Would I had never tried, but lived in hope.   210

191 *closet* private room
196 *tangled* entangled
200 *mere,* sheer, downright
201 *countenance* be in keeping with
209 *strange* distant, stand-offish

184 Mosby's decision to reject Alice might, in performance, be underlined by his
    returning the silver dice, which Alice then returns to him (11. 215–6 below?) as
    a sign of reconciliation. Presumably, it should be these same dice with which
    Mosby and Arden play in Scene XIV.

ALICE

What needs thou try me whom thou never found false?

MOSBY

Yet pardon me, for love is jealous.

ALICE

So lists the sailor to the mermaid's song;
So looks the traveller to the basilisk.
I am content for to be reconciled,   215
And that I know will be mine overthrow.

MOSBY

Thine overthrow? First let the world dissolve!

ALICE

Nay, Mosby, let me still enjoy thy love,
And happen what will, I am resolute.
My saving husband hoards up bags of gold   220
To make our children rich, and now is he
Gone to unload the goods that shall be thine,
And he and Franklin will to London straight.

MOSBY

To London, Alice? If thou'lt be ruled by me,
We'll make him sure enough for coming there.   225

ALICE

Ah, would we could!

MOSBY

I happened on a painter yesternight,
The only cunning man of Christendom,
For he can temper poison with his oil
That whoso looks upon the work he draws   230

---

218 *still* always
223 *straight* straightaway
225 *for* to prevent (him) from (*O.E.D.*, 23. †d.). (See XIV, 223)
228 *only* most
     cunning possessing skill in magic
229 *temper* mix

---

213 The mermaid, often equated in mythology with the Siren, lured sailors to
    destruction with her enchanting and seductive singing.
214 *the basilisk* was a fabulous reptile, hatched by a serpent from a cock's egg,
    whose look alone was fatal.
221 *our children* No children appear in the play, but according to Holinshed, 'After
    supper, mistres Arden caused hir daughter to plaie on the virginals', and he later
    refers to 'one of mistres Ardens owne daughters.' Here, however, I think Alice is
    enjoying the prospect of the children she and Mosby will have being made rich
    by the efforts of the unsuspecting Arden.

Shall, with the beams that issue from his sight,
Suck venom to his breast and slay himself.
Sweet Alice, he shall draw thy counterfeit,
That Arden may by gazing on it perish.
ALICE
Ay, but Mosby, that is dangerous,   235
For thou, or I, or any other else,
Coming into the chamber where it hangs, may die.
MOSBY
Ay, but we'll have it covered with a cloth
And hung up in the study for himself.
ALICE
It may not be, for when the picture's drawn,   240
Arden, I know, will come and show it me.
MOSBY
Fear not; we'll have that shall serve the turn.
This is the painter's house; I'll call him forth.
ALICE
But, Mosby, I'll have no such picture, I.
MOSBY
I pray thee leave it to my discretion.   245
How, Clarke!
                        Here enters CLARKE
Oh, you are an honest man of your word; you served
    me well.
CLARKE
Why sir, I'll do it for you at any time,
Provided, as you have given your word,
I may have Susan Mosby to my wife.   250
For as sharp-witted poets, whose sweet verse
Make heavenly gods break off their nectar draughts
And lay their ears down to the lowly earth,
Use humble promise to their sacred Muse,
So we that are the poets' favourites   255
Must have a love. Ay, love is the painter's Muse,

233 *counterfeit* portrait, likeness
257 *frame* fashion

---

231 It was a contemporary theory that the eyes sent out beams to the object sighted.
243 *the painter's house* probably referring to one of the doors at the rear of the stage.
246 *Clarke* The name is the playwright's invention: the Faversham Wardmote Book
    identifies him as William Blackborne.
251–6 'Just as poets need a Muse to inspire their imaginations to produce their
    finest work . . .so painters need Love to inspire them to theirs.'

That makes him frame a speaking countenance,
A weeping eye that witnesses heart's grief.
Then tell me, Master Mosby, shall I have her?

ALICE
'Tis pity but he should; he'll use her well.   260

MOSBY
Clarke, here's my hand; my sister shall be thine.

CLARKE
Then, brother, to requite this courtesy,
You shall command my life, my skill, and all.

ALICE
Ah, that thou could'st be secret!

MOSBY
Fear him not. Leave; I have talked sufficient.   265

CLARKE
You know not me that ask such questions.
Let it suffice I know you love him well,
And fain would have your husband made away;
Wherein, trust me, you show a noble mind,
That rather than you'll live with him you hate,   270
You'll venture life and die with him you love.
The like will I do for my Susan's sake.

ALICE
Yet nothing could enforce me to the deed
But Mosby's love. Might I without control
Enjoy thee still, then Arden should not die;   275
But seeing I cannot, therefore let him die.

MOSBY
Enough, sweet Alice; thy kind words makes me melt.
[*To* CLARKE] Your trick of poisoned pictures we dislike;
Some other poison would do better far.

ALICE
Ay, such as might be put into his broth,   280
And yet in taste not to be found at all.

CLARKE
I know your mind, and here I have it for you.
Put but a dram of this into his drink,
Or any kind of broth that he shall eat,
And he shall die within an hour after.   285

260 *but* unless
     use treat
268 *fain* willingly, gladly
274 *control* restraint

ALICE

As I am a gentlewoman, Clarke, next day
Thou and Susan shall be married.

MOSBY

And I'll make her dowry more than I'll talk of, Clarke.

CLARKE

Yonder's your husband. Mosby, I'll be gone.

Exit CLARKE

Here enters ARDEN *and* FRANKLIN

ALICE

In good time. See where my husband comes,   290
Master Mosby. Ask him the question yourself.

MOSBY

Master Arden, being at London yesternight,
The Abbey lands whereof you are now possessed
Were offered me on some occasion
By Greene, one of Sir Antony Ager's men.   295
I pray you, sir, tell me, are not the lands yours?
Hath any other interest herein?

ARDEN

Mosby, that question we'll decide anon.
Alice, make ready my breakfast; I must hence.

Exit ALICE

As for the lands, Mosby, they are mine   300

289 s.d. *Exit* CLARKE —after l. 291 in Qq.
294 *occasion* pretext

---

289 s.d. Wine adopts Sturgess' suggestion that Michael should enter with Arden and
Franklin at this point, on the grounds that Arden addresses him at l. 363, and
that Qq indicate he leaves with Arden and Franklin at l. 416. Michael has not
been at the quay with Arden and Franklin, however, and an entrance for him at
l. 289 means he remains on stage for over 70 lines before he has anything
specific to do, while during that time Arden speaks more freely than would seem
likely in the presence of his servant. It is neater if Michael enters with Alice at
1.359, possibly carrying the stools on which Arden and Mosby sit. He could
then either (a) exit after l. 363 and enter again shortly afterwards (possibly on l.
382 while Franklin is giving Arden the mithridate) which may prompt
Franklin's line at 384, or (b) since the pace of this section of the scene means an
entrance might distract attention from the main focus and lessen the tension,
Michael's intended exit at l. 363 could be delayed by Arden's sudden distress,
and he could remain on stage until exiting with Arden and Franklin at l. 416.
290 *In good time* spoken to the departing Clarke.
290–1 *See . . .yourself* Alice speaks these lines for Arden to hear, in order to allay his
suspicions at finding her with Mosby. Mosby understands immediately, and
responds accordingly.
295 *Sir Anthony Ager* in reality, Sir Anthony Aucher, a knight of Hautsbourne in
Kent.

By letters patents from his majesty.
But I must have a mandate for my wife;
They say you seek to rob me of her love.
Villain, what makes thou in her company?
She's no companion for so base a groom.   305
MOSBY
Arden, I thought not on her, I came to thee;
But rather than I pocket up this wrong—
FRANKLIN
What will you do, sir?
MOSBY
Revenge it on the proudest of you both.
          Then ARDEN *draws forth* MOSBY'S *sword*
ARDEN
So, sirrah, you may not wear a sword.   310
The statute makes against artificers,
I warrant that I do. Now use your bodkin,
Your Spanish needle, and your pressing iron,
For this shall go with me. And mark my words,
You goodman botcher, 'tis to you I speak: 315

302 *mandate* deed of ownership
305 *groom* serving man (cf. I. 25–30)
307 *pocket up* accept without showing resentment, 'swallow'
311 *makes* decrees

---

310 *sirrah* 'A term of address. . .expressing contempt, reprimand, or assumption of
     authority on the part of the speaker' (*O.E.D.*).
311 *statute* passed under Edward III, forbidding anyone under the rank of
     gentleman from wearing a sword.
     artificers craftsmen (though *O.E.D.* †6., notes that the word also had the
     contemporary meaning of 'a trickster').
312 *I . . .do* I have warrant for what I do.
313 *Spanish needle* an embroidery needle, used for fine 'Spanish work', or 'Black
     work', embroidery in black silk which was in the height of fashion between
     1570–90 (M. Channing Linthicum, *Costume in Elizabethan Drama,* Oxford,
     1936, pp. 149–50). In view of Arden's charge that Mosby is only a *botcher,* this
     jibe is carefully aimed.
315 *goodman* prefixed (sometimes with ironical intention) to the names of those
     beneath the rank of gentleman.

The next time that I take thee near my house,
Instead of legs I'll make thee crawl on stumps.
MOSBY
Ah, Master Arden, you have injured me;
I do appeal to God and to the world.
FRANKLIN
Why, canst thou deny wert a botcher once?   320
MOSBY
Measure me what I am, not what I was.
ARDEN
Why, what art thou now but a velvet drudge,
A cheating steward, and base-minded peasant?
MOSBY
Arden, now thou hast belched and vomited
The rancorous venom of thy mis-swoll'n heart,   325
Hear me but speak. As I intend to live
With God and His elected saints in heaven,
I never meant more to solicit her;
And that she knows, and all the world shall see.
I loved her once—sweet Arden, pardon me.   330
I could not choose, her beauty fired my heart.
But time hath quenched these over-raging coals,
And, Arden, though I now frequent thy house,
'Tis for my sister's sake, her waiting-maid,
And not for hers. Mayest thou enjoy her long;   335
Hell-fire and wrathful vengeance light on me
If I dishonour her or injure thee.
ARDEN
Mosby, with these thy protestations
The deadly hatred of my heart is appeased,
And thou and I'll be friends if this prove true.   340
As for the base terms I gave thee late,
Forget them, Mosby; I had cause to speak
When all the knights and gentlemen of Kent
Make common table-talk of her and thee.
MOSBY
Who lives that is not touched with slanderous tongues?   345
FRANKLIN
Then, Mosby, to eschew the speech of men,

[handwritten margin note: connection between men is most important.]

322 *velvet drudge* menial in velvet livery
341 *late* just now

Upon whose general bruit all honour hangs,
Forbear his house.

ARDEN

Forbear it! Nay, rather frequent it more.
The world shall see that I distrust her not.   350
To warn him on the sudden from my house
Were to confirm the rumour that is grown.

MOSBY

By my faith, sir, you say true,
And therefore will I sojourn here awhile
Until our enemies have talked their fill;   355
And then, I hope, they'll cease and at last confess
How causeless they have injured her and me.

ARDEN

And I will lie at London all this term
To let them see how light I weigh their words.

Here enters ALICE [*and* MICHAEL]

ALICE

Husband, sit down; your breakfast will be cold.   360

ARDEN

Come, Master Mosby, will you sit with us?

MOSBY

I cannot eat, but I'll sit for company.

ARDEN

Sirrah Michael, see our horse be ready.   [? *Exit* MICHAEL]

ALICE

Husband, why pause ye? Why eat you not?

ARDEN

I am not well; there's something in this broth   365
That is not wholesome. Didst thou make it, Alice?

ALICE

I did, and that's the cause it likes not you.

Then she throws down the broth on the ground

There's nothing that I do can please your taste.
You were best to say I would have poisoned you.
I cannot speak or cast aside my eye,   370
But he imagines I have stepped awry.
Here's he that you cast in my teeth so oft;

347 *bruit* report, opinion
353 *my faith* ed. (faith my Qq)
367 *likes not you* displeases you, offends you

359, 363, 382 s.d.s See note to 1. 289 s.d.

[handwritten annotation:] women and supposed to cook

[handwritten annotation:] villians manipulate cultural codes by standing outside of them · she plays a role.

+ manipulating cultural codes of femininity

Now will I be convinced or purge myself.
I charge thee speak to this mistrustful man,
Thou that wouldst see me hang, thou, Mosby, thou. 375
What favour hast thou had more than a kiss
At coming or departing from the town?

MOSBY

You wrong yourself and me to cast these doubts;
Your loving husband is not jealous.

ARDEN

Why, gentle Mistress Alice, cannot I be ill 380
But you'll accuse yourself?
Franklin, thou has a box of mithridate;

[?*Enter* MICHAEL]

I'll take a little to prevent the worst.

FRANKLIN

Do so, and let us presently take horse.
My life for yours, ye shall do well enough. 385

ALICE

Give me a spoon; I'll eat of it myself.
Would it were full of poison to the brim!
Then should my cares and troubles have an end.
Was ever silly woman so tormented?

ARDEN

Be patient, sweet love; I mistrust not thee. 390

ALICE

God will revenge it, Arden, if thou dost,
For never woman loved her husband better
Than I do thee.

ARDEN

I know it, sweet Alice; cease to complain,
Lest that in tears I answer thee again. 395

FRANKLIN

Come, leave this dallying, and let us away.

ALICE

Forbear to wound me with that bitter word.
Arden shall go to London in my arms.

ARDEN

Loth am I to depart, yet I must go.

373 *convinced* proved guilty
389 *silly* helpless, defenceless

---

382 *mithridate* a universal antidote, 'so called from Mithridates VI, king of Pontus
(died *c.* 63 B.C.), who was said to have rendered himself proof against poisons by
the constant use of antidotes' (*O.E.D.*).

ALICE

Wilt thou to London, then, and leave me here?   400
Ah, if thou love me, gentle Arden, stay.
Yet if thy business be of great import,
Go if thou wilt; I'll bear it as I may.
But write from London to me every week,
Nay, every day, and stay no longer there   405
Than thou must needs, lest that I die for sorrow.

ARDEN

I'll write unto thee every other tide,
And so farewell, sweet Alice, till we meet next.

ALICE

Farewell, husband, seeing you'll have it so.
And, Master Franklin, seeing you take him hence,   410
In hope you'll hasten him home I'll give you this.
            And then she kisseth him

FRANKLIN

And if he stay the fault shall not be mine.
Mosby, farewell, and see you keep your oath.

MOSBY

I hope he is not jealous of me now.

ARDEN

No, Mosby, no; hereafter think of me   415
As of your dearest friend. And so farewell.
            Exeunt ARDEN, FRANKLIN *and* MICHAEL

ALICE

I am glad he is gone; he was about to stay,
But did you mark me then how I brake off?

MOSBY

Ay, Alice, and it was cunningly performed.
But what a villain is this painter Clarke!   420

ALICE

Was it not a goodly poison that he gave!
Why, he's as well now as he was before.
It should have been some fine confection
That might have given the broth some dainty taste.
This powder was too gross and populous.   425

MOSBY

But had he eaten but three spoonfuls more,
Then had he died and our love continued.

423 *confection* 1. mixture, compound 2. deadly poison
425 *gross and populous* indigestible and perceptible (Wine)

411 Cf. I, 376–7.

ALICE
Why, so it shall, Mosby, albeit he live.

MOSBY
It is unpossible, for I have sworn
Never hereafter to solicit thee   430
Or, whilst he lives, once more importune thee.

ALICE
Thou shalt not need; I will importune thee.
What, shall an oath make thee forsake my love?
As if I have not sworn as much myself,
And given my hand unto him in the church!   435
Tush, Mosby. Oaths are words, and words is wind,
And wind is mutable. Then I conclude
'Tis childishness to stand upon an oath.

MOSBY
Well proved, Mistress Alice; yet, by your leave,
I'll keep mine unbroken whilst he lives.   440

ALICE
Ay, do, and spare not. His time is but short,
For if thou beest as resolute as I,
We'll have him murdered as he walks the streets.
In London many alehouse ruffians keep,
Which, as I hear, will murder men for gold.   445
They shall be soundly fee'd to pay him home.
                    Here enters GREENE

MOSBY
Alice, what's he that comes yonder? Knowest thou him?

ALICE
Mosby, be gone. I hope 'tis one that comes
To put in practice our intended drifts.   *Exit* MOSBY

GREENE
Mistress Arden, you are well met.   450
I am sorry that your husband is from home
Whenas my purposed journey was to him.
Yet all my labour is not spent in vain,
For I suppose that you can full discourse
And flat resolve me of the thing I seek.   455

ALICE
What is it, Master Greene? If that I may
Or can with safety, I will answer you.

444 *keep* lodge, live
446 *to pay him home* i.e. to kill him
454 *full discourse* fully explain
455 *flat resolve* make completely clear to

GREENE

    I heard your husband hath the grant of late,
    Confirmed by letters patents from the king,
    Of all of the lands of the Abbey of Faversham,   460
    Generally intitled, so that all former grants
    Are cut off, whereof I myself had one;
    But now my interest by that is void.
    This is all, Mistress Arden; is it true nor no?

ALICE

    True, Master Greene; the lands are his in state,   465
    And whatsoever leases were before
    Are void for term of Master Arden's life.
    He hath the grant under the Chancery seal.

GREENE

    Pardon me, Mistress Arden; I must speak
    For I am touched. Your husband doth me wrong   470
    To wring me from the little land I have.
    My living is my life; only that
    Resteth remainder of my portion.
    Desire of wealth is endless in his mind,
    And he is greedy-gaping still for gain.   475
    Nor cares he though young gentlemen do beg,
    So he may scrape and hoard up in his pouch.
    But seeing he hath taken my lands, I'll value life
    As careless as he is careful for to get;
    And tell him this from me: I'll be revenged,   480
    And so as he shall wish the Abbey lands
    Had rested still within their former state.

ALICE

    Alas, poor gentleman, I pity you,
    And woe is me that any man should want.
    God knows, 'tis not my fault. But wonder not   485

---

461 *Generally intitled* deeded without any exceptions
465 *in state* by law (see XIII, 19–20, and Intro., p. xxviii)
467 *term* the duration
470 *touched* affected, disturbed
472 *living* property, land
472-3 *only . . .portion* only my land remains of what I inherited
475 *still* always
477 *So* so long as

---

468 The Court of the Lord Chancellor was the highest in the land, next to the House of Lords.

Though he be hard to others when to me—
Ah, Master Greene, God knows how I am used!

GREENE

Why, Mistress Arden, can the crabbed churl
Use you unkindly? Respects he not your birth,
Your honourable friends, nor what you brought?   490
Why, all Kent knows your parentage and what you are.

ALICE

Ah, Master Greene, be it spoken in secret here,
I never live good day with him alone.
When he is at home, then have I froward looks,
Hard words, and blows to mend the match withal.   495
And though I might content as good a man,
Yet doth he keep in every corner trulls;
And weary with his trugs at home,
Then rides he straight to London; there, forsooth,
He revels it among such filthy ones   500
As counsels him to make away his wife.
Thus live I daily in continual fear,
In sorrow, so despairing of redress
As every day I wish with hearty prayer
That he or I were taken forth the world.   505

GREENE

Now trust me, Mistress Alice, it grieveth me
So fair a creature should be so abused.
Why, who would have thought the civil sir so sullen?
He looks so smoothly. Now, fie upon him, churl!
And if he live a day he lives too long.   510
But frolic, woman; I shall be the man
Shall set you free from all this discontent.
And if the churl deny my interest,
And will not yield my lease into my hand,
I'll pay him home, whatever hap to me.   515

ALICE

But speak you as you think?

488 *crabbed* ill-natured
490 *what you brought* i.e. your dowry
494 *froward* bad tempered
495 *mend the match* make up the marriage bargain (Sturgess)
497, 8 *trulls, trugs* whores, prostitutes
509 *smoothly* courteous
511 *frolic* cheer up
513 *interest* legal right to property

GREENE

    Ay, God's my witness, I mean plain dealing,
    For I had rather die than lose my land.

ALICE

    Then, Master Greene, be counselled by me:
    Endanger not yourself for such a churl,   520
    But hire some cutter for to cut him short;
    And here's ten pound to wager them withal.
    When he is dead you shall have twenty more,
    And the lands whereof my husband is possessed
    Shall be intitled as they were before.   525

GREENE

    Will you keep promise with me?

ALICE

    Or count me false and perjured whilst I live.

GREENE

    Then here's my hand, I'll have him so dispatched.
    I'll up to London straight; I'll thither post,
    And never rest till I have compassed it.   530
    Till then farewell.

ALICE

    Good fortune follow all your forward thoughts.

                                     Exit GREENE

    And whosoever doth attempt the deed
    A happy hand I wish, and so farewell.
    All this goes well. Mosby, I long for thee   535
    To let thee know all that I have contrived.

                 Here enters MOSBY *and* CLARKE

MOSBY

    How now, Alice, what's the news?

ALICE

    Such as will content thee well, sweetheart.

MOSBY

    Well, let them pass awhile, and tell me, Alice,
    How have you dealt and tempered with my sister?   540
    What, will she have my neighbour Clarke or no?

521 *cutter* cut-throat
522 *wager* pay
529 *post* travel without delay
532 *forward* eager
539 *them* i.e. the news
540 *tempered with* persuaded

ALICE

What, Master Mosby! Let him woo himself.
Think you that maids look not for fair words?
Go to her, Clarke, she's all alone within.
Michael, my man, is clean out of her books. 545

CLARKE

I thank you, Mistress Arden, I will in,
And if fair Susan and I can make a gree,
You shall command me to the uttermost,
As far as either goods or life may stretch. *Exit* CLARKE

MOSBY

Now, Alice, let's hear thy news. 550

ALICE

They be so good that I must laugh for joy
Before I can begin to tell my tale.

MOSBY

Let's hear them, that I may laugh for company.

ALICE

This morning, Master Greene—Dick Greene, I mean,
From whom my husband had the Abbey land— 555
Came hither railing for to know the truth,
Whether my husband had the lands by grant.
I told him all, whereat he stormed amain
And swore he would cry quittance with the churl
And, if he did deny his interest, 560
Stab him, whatsoever did befall himself.
Whenas I saw his choler thus to rise,
I whetted on the gentleman with words,
And, to conclude, Mosby, at last we grew
To composition for my husband's death. 565
I gave him ten pound to hire knaves
By some device to make away the churl.
When he is dead he should have twenty more
And repossess his former lands again.
On this we 'greed, and he is ridden straight 570
To London to bring his death about.

MOSBY

But call you this good news?

547 *make a gree* come to terms
558 *amain* vehemently, violently
559 *cry quittance with* get even with
563 *whetted on* incited
565 *composition* agreement (for payment)

ALICE

Ay, sweetheart, be they not?

MOSBY

'Twere cheerful news to hear the churl were dead,
But trust me, Alice, I take it passing ill   575
You would be so forgetful of our state
To make recount of it to every groom.
What! to acquaint each stranger with our drifts,
Chiefly in case of murder! Why, 'tis the way
To make it open unto Arden's self,   580
And bring thyself and me to ruin both.
Forewarned, forearmed; who threats his enemy
Lends him a sword to guard himself withal.

ALICE

I did it for the best.

MOSBY

Well, seeing 'tis done, cheerly let it pass.   585
You know this Greene; is he not religious?
A man, I guess, of great devotion?

ALICE

He is.

MOSBY

Then, sweet Alice, let it pass. I have a drift
Will quiet all, whatever is amiss.   590

Here enters CLARKE *and* SUSAN

ALICE

How now, Clarke, have you found me false?
Did I not plead the matter hard for you?

CLARKE

You did.

MOSBY

And what? Will't be a match?

CLARKE

A match, i'faith, sir. Ay, the day is mine.   595
The painter lays his colours to the life,
His pencil draws no shadows in his love;
Susan is mine.

ALICE

You make her blush.

575 *passing* extremely

586–7 See Intro., p. xx.
596–7 'The painter reproduces life faithfully, and, in this case, his pencil need draw
    no shadows in his love.' (?)

MOSBY
What, sister, is it Clarke must be the man?   600
SUSAN
It resteth in your grant. Some words are passed,
And haply we be grown unto a match
If you be willing that it shall be so.
MOSBY
Ah, Master Clarke, it resteth at my grant;
You see my sister's yet at my dispose.   605
But, so you'll grant me one thing I shall ask,
I am content my sister shall be yours.
CLARKE
What is it, Master Mosby?
MOSBY
I do remember once in secret talk
You told me how you could compound by art   610
A crucifix impoisoned,
That whoso look upon it should wax blind,
And with the scent be stifled, that ere long
He should die poisoned that did view it well.
I would have you make me such a crucifix,   615
And then I'll grant my sister shall be yours.
CLARKE
Though I am loth, because it toucheth life,
Yet rather or I'll leave sweet Susan's love
I'll do it, and with all the haste I may.
But for whom is it?   620
ALICE
Leave that to us. Why, Clarke, is it possible
That you should paint and draw it out yourself,
The colours being baleful and impoisoned,
And no ways prejudice yourself withal?
MOSBY
Well questioned, Alice. Clarke, how answer you that?   625
CLARKE
Very easily. I'll tell you straight
How I do work of these impoisoned drugs:
I fasten on my spectacles so close
As nothing can any way offend my sight;
Then, as I put a leaf within my nose,   630

602 *haply* perhaps   624 *prejudice* endanger
618 *or* than   629 *offend* damage
623 *baleful* noxious, harmful

So put I rhubarb to avoid the smell,
And softly as another work I paint.

MOSBY
'Tis very well, but against when shall I have it?

CLARKE
Within this ten days.

MOSBY
'Twill serve the turn.
Now, Alice, let's in and see what cheer you keep.   635
                                            [*Exit* CLARKE]
I hope now Master Arden is from home,
You'll give me leave to play your husband's part.

ALICE
Mosby, you know who's master of my heart;
He well may be the master of the house.   *Exeunt*   640

Scene II

Here enters GREENE *and* BRADSHAW

BRADSHAW
See you them that comes yonder, Master Greene?

GREENE
Ay, very well. Do you know them?
                Here enters BLACK WILL *and* SHAKEBAG

BRADSHAW
The one I know not, but he seems a knave,
Chiefly for bearing the other company;
For such a slave, so vile a rogue as he,   5
Lives not again upon the earth.
Black Will is his name. I tell you, Master Greene,
At Boulogne he and I were fellow soldiers,
Where he played such pranks
As all the camp feared him for his villainy.   10
I warrant you he bears so bad a mind
That for a crown he'll murder any man.

GREENE [*Aside*]
The fitter is he for my purpose, marry!

BLACK WILL
How now, fellow Bradshaw! Whither away so early?

632 *softly as another* as easily as with any other   11 *warrant* assure

---

631 *rhubarb* believed to have medicinal properties, and used as a purgative drug.

8 *Boulogne* French port on the English Channel. It was captured by Henry VIII in
1544, and restored to France by Edward VI in 1550.

BRADSHAW

    Oh, Will, times are changed; no fellows now,   15
    Though we were once together in the field;
    Yet thy friend to do thee any good I can.

BLACK WILL

    Why, Bradshaw, was not thou and I fellow soldiers at
    Boulogne, where I was a corporal and thou but a base
    mercenary groom? 'No fellows now' because you are a   20
    goldsmith and have a little plate in your shop? You were glad
    to call me 'fellow Will' and, with a curtsey to the earth, 'one
    snatch, good corporal', when I stole the half ox from John
    the victualler, and domineered with it amongst good fellows
    in one night.   25

BRADSHAW

    Ay, Will, those days are past with me.

BLACK WILL

    Ay, but they be not past with me, for I keep that same
    honourable mind still. Good neighbour Bradshaw, you are
    too proud to be my fellow, but were it not that I see more
    company coming down the hill, I would be fellows with you   30
    once more, and share crowns with you too. But let that pass,
    and tell me whither you go.

BRADSHAW

    To London, Will, about a piece of service
    Wherein haply thou may'st pleasure me.

BLACK WILL

    What is it?   35

BRADSHAW

    Of late, Lord Cheiny lost some plate,

---

22 *curtsey* ed. (cursy Qq) bow   24 *domineered* revelled
23 *snatch* morsel   31 *share crowns with you* i.e. rob you

---

13 *marry!* an oath derived from the name of the Virgin Mary.

36–69 It has been suggested that the episode has local relevance and indicates either
    that the author was from Kent, or that the lines were added to the prompt copy
    by the actors who were touring the play in that county.
       It serves, however, a number of important dramatic functions; firstly, it
    allows Greene time to compose the letter to Alice (see VIII, 153–60, and XVIII,
    2–7); secondly, it skilfully establishes the new characters of Black Will and
    Shakebag; and thirdly, if, as seems likely (the striking physical description
    Bradshaw gives of Fitten would scarcely seem to require the further details of
    his apparel), Black Will is deliberately spinning out the time before he reveals
    Fitten's name, making Bradshaw pay up while he does so, it establishes
    Bradshaw as an innocent man used by others, a role he plays with fatal results.

Which one did bring and sold it at my shop,
Saying he served Sir Antony Cooke.
A search was made, the plate was found with me,
And I am bound to answer at the 'size.   40
Now Lord Cheiny solemnly vows,
If law will serve him, he'll hang me for his plate.
Now I am going to London upon hope
To find the fellow. Now, Will, I know
Thou art acquainted with such companions.   45

BLACK WILL
What manner of man was he?

BRADSHAW
A lean-faced, writhen knave,
Hawk-nosed and very hollow-eyed,
With mighty furrows in his stormy brows,
Long hair down his shoulders curled;   50
His chin was bare, but on his upper lip
A mutchado, which he wound about his ear.

BLACK WILL
What apparel had he?

BRADSHAW
A watchet satin doublet all to-torn
(The inner side did bear the greater show),   55
A pair of threadbare velvet hose, seam rent,
A worsted stocking rent above the shoe,
A livery cloak, but all the lace was off;
'Twas bad, but yet it served to hide the plate.

38 *Sir Anthony Cooke* (1504–76) tutor to Edward VI.
40 *'size* assize (usually in plural)
47 *writhen* cringing, twisted
52 *mutchado* moustache
54 *watchet* light blue
   all to-torn completely torn
55 *The . . .show* more of the lining than the outside was visible
57 *worsted* ed. (wosted Q1, 3; wosten Q2)

BLACK WILL

    Sirrah Shakebag, canst thou remember since we trolled the   60
bowl at Sittingburgh, where I broke the tapster's head of the
Lion with a cudgel-stick?

SHAKEBAG

    Ay, very well, Will.

BLACK WILL

    Why, it was with the money that the plate was sold for.
Sirrah Bradshaw, what wilt thou give him that can tell thee   65
who sold thy plate?

BRADSHAW

    Who, I pray thee, good Will?

BLACK WILL

    Why, 'twas one Jack Fitten. He's now in Newgate for
stealing a horse, and shall be arraigned the next 'size.

BRADSHAW

    Why then, let Lord Cheiny seek Jack Fitten forth,   70
For I'll back and tell him who robbed him of his plate.
This cheers my heart. Master Greene, I'll leave you,
For I must to the Isle of Sheppey with speed.

GREENE

    Before you go, let me entreat you
To carry this letter to Mistress Arden of Faversham   75
And humbly recommend me to herself.

BRADSHAW

    That will I, Master Greene, and so farewell.
Here, Will, there's a crown for thy good news.

                             Exit BRADSHAW

BLACK WILL

    Farewell, Bradshaw; I'll drink no water for thy sake whilst
this lasts. Now, gentleman, shall we have your company to   80
London?

60–1 *trolled the bowl* passed round the drinking cup, celebrated
69 *arraigned* indicted, charged

---

61 *Sittingburgh* i.e. Sittingbourne, a town in Kent about 9 miles east of Faversham.
    (See map.)
61–2 *tapster's head of the Lion* i.e., the head of the tapster (barman) at the Lion
    Inn.
68 *Newgate* The 'chief prison of London. Those who were condemned to death
    were carted out to Tyburn for execution: the dismal procession passed by St.
    Sepulchre's church, where a nosegay was given to the condemned man'
    (Sugden).
73 *Isle of Sheppey* 'an island in Kent, separated from the mainland by a branch of
    the Medway . . . .just opposite to Faversham' (Sugden). (See map.)

GREENE

Nay, stay, sirs,
A little more: I needs must use your help,
And in a matter of great consequence,
Wherein if you'll be secret and profound,　　　　85
I'll give you twenty angels for your pains.

BLACK WILL

How? Twenty angels? Give my fellow George Shakebag and
me twenty angels, and if thou'lt have thy own father slain
that thou mayest inherit his land we'll kill him.

SHAKEBAG

Ay, thy mother, thy sister, thy brother, or all thy kin.　　90

GREENE

Well, this it is: Arden of Faversham
Hath highly wronged me about the Abbey land,
That no no revenge but death will serve the turn.
Will you two kill him? Here's the angels down,
And I will lay the platform of his death.　　　　95

BLACK WILL

Plat me no platforms! Give me the money and I'll stab him
as he stands pissing against a wall, but I'll kill him.

SHAKEBAG

Where is he?

GREENE

He is now at London, in Aldersgate Street.

SHAKEBAG

He's dead as if he had been condemned by an Act of　100
Parliament if once Black Will and I swear his death.

GREENE

Here is ten pound, and when he is dead
Ye shall have twenty more.

BLACK WILL

My fingers itches to be at the peasant. Ah, that I might be set

---

85 *profound* cunning
95 *lay the platform* devise the plan

---

86 *angels* gold coins worth about 10 shillings. They were embossed with the device
of the Archangel Michael slaying the dragon.
99 *Aldersgate Street* ran south from Aldersgate 'to St. Martin's-le-Grand, and so
into the west end of Cheapside ... the town houses of the Earls of
Northumberland, Westmorland, and Thanet, and of the Marquis of Dorchester,
were in this street' (Sugden). See Intro., p. xxii – xxiv.

a work thus through the year and that murder would grow to   105
an occupation that a man might without danger of law.
Zounds! I warrant I should be warden of the company.
Come, let us be going, and we'll bait at Rochester, where I'll
give thee a gallon of sack to handsel the match withal.

Exeunt

Scene III

Here enters MICHAEL

MICHAEL
   I have gotten such a letter as will touch the painter, and thus
it is:
> *Here enters* ARDEN *and* FRANKLIN *and hears*
> MICHAEL *read this letter*
'My duty remembered, Mistress Susan, hoping in God you
be in good health, as I, Michael, was at the making hereof.
This is to certify you that, as the turtle true, when she hath   5
lost her mate, sitteth alone, so I, mourning for your absence,
do walk up and down Paul's till one day I fell asleep and lost

---

108 *bait* stop for food and rest
109 *handsel* seal with success

5 *certify* assure
   turtle turtle dove

---

106 *might* i.e., might follow it.
107 *Zounds!* oath derived from 'By God's wounds'.
   warden of the company Black Will imagines a company dealing in murder and
   extortion (see XIV, 5–28) being established as one of the legitimate Livery
   Companies of the City of London, with himself as *warden* (that is, the governor,
   or member of the governing body) of the company.
108 *Rochester* 'ancient episcopal city in Kent, on the Medway, 33 miles east of
   London' (Sugden). (See map.)
109 *sack* white wine, imported from Spain and the Canaries.

3-15 Michael's letter is clearly a parody of the euphuistic style (named after John
   Lyly's *Euphues, The Anatomy of Wit,* 1578, and *Euphues and His England,*
   1580), with its elaborate rhetorical devices and sentence structure, similes,
   word-play, proverbs, and fables. Here, obviously, the comic effect is achieved by
   the stark contrast between the form and the actual content of the letter.
7 *Paul's* i.e., St Paul's Cathedral in London. The middle aisle of the Cathedral,
   known as Paul's Walk (or Duke Humphrey's Walk), was a popular meeting-
   place for merchants and businessmen, as well as being the haunt of prostitutes
   and pickpockets (see 11.47–48).

my master's pantofles. Ah, Mistress Susan, abolish that
paltry painter, cut him off by the shins with a frowning look
of your crabbed countenance, and think upon Michael, who,   10
drunk with the dregs of your favour, will cleave as fast to
your love as a plaster of pitch to a galled horseback. Thus
hoping you will let my passions penetrate, or rather
impetrate, mercy of your meek hands, I end.
                    Yours, Michael, or else not Michael.'   15

ARDEN
Why, you paltry knave!
Stand you here loitering, knowing my affairs,
What haste my business craves to send to Kent?

FRANKLIN
'Faith, friend Michael, this is very ill,
Knowing your master hath no more but you,   20
And do ye slack his business for your own?

ARDEN
Where is the letter, sirrah? Let me see it.
                    Then he [MICHAEL] *gives him the letter*
See, Master Franklin, here's proper stuff:
Susan my maid, the painter, and my man,
A crew of harlots, all in love, forsooth.   25
Sirrah, let me hear no more of this,
Nor, for thy life, once write to her a word.
                    Here enters GREENE, [BLACK] WILL, *and* SHAKEBAG
Wilt thou be married to so base a trull?
'Tis Mosby's sister. Come I once at home
I'll rouse her from remaining in my house.   30
Now, Master Franklin, let us go walk in Paul's.
Come, but a turn or two and then away.
                    Exeunt [ARDEN, FRANKLIN, *and* MICHAEL]

---

13 *galled* sore with chafing
14 *impetrate* obtain by request, beseech
18 *send* i.e. to be sent
25 *harlots* lewd persons of either sex
27 *Nor* ed. (Now Qq)

---

8 *pantofles* overshoes or galoshes; presumably entrusted to Michael's care while
   Arden was inside the Cathedral doing business.
12 *plaster . . .horseback* 'part of a remedy suggested by Nicholas Maltby (supposed
   author) in *Remedies for diseases in Horses* (London, 1576)' (Wine).

GREENE

The first is Arden, and that's his man.
The other is Franklin, Arden's dearest friend.

BLACK WILL

Zounds, I'll kill them all three.   35

GREENE

Nay, sirs, touch not his man in any case;
But stand close and take you fittest standing,
And at his coming forth speed him.
To the Nag's Head, there is this coward's haunt.
But now I'll leave you till the deed be done.   40

Exit GREENE

SHAKEBAG

If he be not paid his own, ne'er trust Shakebag.

BLACK WILL

Sirrah Shakebag, at his coming forth I'll run him through,
and then to the Blackfriars and there take water and away.

SHAKEBAG

Why, that's the best; but see thou miss him not.

BLACK WILL

How can I miss him, when I think on the forty angels I must   45
have more?

Here enters a PRENTICE

37 *stand close* conceal yourselves
38 *speed* kill, dispatch
41 *paid his own* i.e. killed
43 *take water* take a boat across the Thames

---

37 *fittest standing* best position (with the sense, as it is used specifically in IX, 38, of
a 'stand from which to shoot game', which ties in with the hunting imagery and
terminology which runs through the play.) *O.E.D.* also notes that *standing* can
refer to the position occupied by a stall, or to the stall itself.
39 *Nag's Head* 'A·tavern in London, at the East corner of Cheapside and Friday
Street' (Sugden).
43 *Blackfriars* A fashionable district of London which retained the right of
sanctuary even after the dissolution of the Dominican monastery in 1538.

PRENTICE

'Tis very late; I were best shut up my stall, for here will be
old filching when the press comes forth of Paul's.

> *Then lets he down his window, and it breaks*
> BLACK WILL.'s *head*

BLACK WILL

Zounds! Draw, Shakebag, draw! I am almost killed.

PRENTICE

We'll tame you, I warrant.   50

BLACK WILL

Zounds, I am tame enough already.

> *Here enters* ARDEN, FRANKLIN, *and* MICHAEL

ARDEN

What troublesome fray or mutiny is this?

FRANKLIN

'Tis nothing but some brabbling, paltry fray,
Devised to pick men's pockets in the throng.

ARDEN

Is't nothing else? Come, Franklin, let us away.   55

> *Exeunt* [ARDEN, FRANKLIN, *and* MICHAEL]

BLACK WILL

What 'mends shall I have for my broken head?

PRENTICE

Marry, this 'mends, that if you get you not away all the
sooner, you shall be well beaten and sent to the Counter.

> *Exit* PRENTICE

BLACK WILL

Well, I'll be gone; but look to your signs, for I'll pull them

---

48 *old filching* much pilfering	51 *tame* hurt
press crowd	53 *brabbling* riotous, brawling
s.d. *breaks* grazes, bruises	56 *'mends* cure, reparation

---

47 *stall* i.e., book stall. St Paul's churchyard was a centre for selling books, and the
sellers' stocks were stored in the vaults of the Cathedral. The title-page of the
1592 Quarto of *Arden* (see p. 1) indicates that its publisher, Edward White, had
his business at 'the lyttle North dore of Paules Church at the signe of the Gun',
and the title-page itself with its lurid and selective account of the play's
contents would have been displayed on the front of the stall to arouse the
interest of potential customers.

48 s.d. A simple structure resembling a book-seller's stall, and incorporating a
practical window or shutter which could be 'let down' is needed here, and
would probably be brought on stage for this scene only.

58 *Counter* a London prison.

down all. Shakebag, my broken head grieves me not so much 60
as by this means Arden hath escaped.

Here enters GREENE

I had a glimpse of him and his companion.

GREENE

Why, sirs, Arden's as well as I; I met him and Franklin going
merrily to the ordinary. What, dare you not do it?

BLACK WILL

Yes, sir, we dare do it; but were my consent to give again we 65
would not do it under ten pound more. I value every drop of
my blood at a French crown. I have had ten pound to steal a
dog, and we have no more here to kill a man. But that a
bargain is a bargain and so forth, you should do it yourself.

GREENE

I pray thee, how came thy head broke? 70

BLACK WILL

Why, thou seest it is broke, dost thou not?

SHAKEBAG

Standing against a stall, watching Arden's coming, a boy let
down his shop window and broke his head; whereupon arose
a brawl, and in the tumult Arden escaped us and passed by
unthought on. But forbearance is no acquittance; another 75
time we'll do it, I warrant thee.

GREENE

I pray thee, Will, make clean thy bloody brow,
And let us bethink us on some other place
Where Arden may be met with handsomely.
Remember how devoutly thou hast sworn 80
To kill the villain; think upon thine oath.

BLACK WILL

Tush, I have broken five hundred oaths!
But wouldst thou charm me to effect this deed,
Tell me of gold, my resolution's fee;
Say thou seest Mosby kneeling at my knees, 85

61 *as* as the fact that
79 *handsomely* conveniently

---

64 *ordinary* a tavern, or its dining room, where meals were provided at a fixed
 price, e.g., 18 pence, as at 1. 124.
85-7 These lines (see also 11.113–6 below), where a character possesses
 unexpected information or knowledge, or (see 1.33 and 1.123 in this scene)
 where there appears to be an inconsistency, may be, as Wine notes, signs of
 authorial confusion or textual corruption, but (unlike the letter in Scene VIII,
 157n) they are unlikely to trouble an audience.

Off'ring me service for my high attempt;
And sweet Alice Arden, with a lap of crowns,
Comes with a lowly curtsey to the earth,
Saying 'Take this but for thy quarterage;
Such yearly tribute will I answer thee.'   90
Why, this would steel soft-mettled cowardice,
With which Black Will was never tainted with.
I tell thee, Greene, the forlorn traveller,
Whose lips are glued with summer's parching heat,
Ne'er longed so much to see a running brook   95
As I to finish Arden's tragedy.
Seest thou this gore that cleaveth to my face?
From hence ne'er will I wash this bloody stain
Till Arden's heart be panting in my hand.

GREENE
Why, that's well said; but what saith Shakebag?   100

SHAKEBAG
I cannot paint my valour out with words;
But give me place and opportunity,
Such mercy as the starven lioness,
When she is dry-sucked of her eager young,
Shows to the prey that next encounters her,   105
On Arden so much pity would I take.

GREENE
So should it fare with men of firm resolve.
And now, sirs, seeing this accident
Of meeting him in Paul's hath no success,
Let us bethink us on some other place   110
Whose earth may swallow up this Arden's blood.

Here enters MICHAEL

See, yonder comes his man. And wot you what?
The foolish knave is in love with Mosby's sister,
And for her sake, whose love he cannot get
Unless Mosby solicit his suit,   115
The villain hath sworn the slaughter of his master.
We'll question him, for he may stead us much.
How now, Michael, whither are you going?

MICHAEL
My master hath new supped,
And I am going to prepare his chamber.   120

---

89 *quarterage* quarterly payment
90 *answer* guarantee
117 *stead us much* give us useful information

GREENE

Where supped Master Arden?

MICHAEL

At the Nag's Head, at the eighteen pence ordinary. How
now, Master Shakebag! What, Black Will! God's dear lady,
how chance your face is so bloody?

BLACK WILL

Go to, sirrah; there is a chance in it this sauciness in you will   125
make you be knocked.

MICHAEL

Nay, and you be offended, I'll be gone.

GREENE

Stay, Michael, you may not 'scape us so.
Michael, I know you love your master well.

MICHAEL

Why, so I do; but wherefore urge you that?   130

GREENE

Because I think you love your mistress better.

MICHAEL

So think not I. But say, i'faith, what if I should?

SHAKEBAG

Come to the purpose. Michael, we hear
You have a pretty love in Faversham.

MICHAEL

Why, have I two or three, what's that to thee?   135

BLACK WILL

You deal too mildly with the peasant. Thus it is:
'Tis known to us you love Mosby's sister;
We know besides that you have ta'en your oath
To further Mosby to your mistress' bed
And kill your master for his sister's sake.   140
Now, sir, a poorer coward than yourself
Was never fostered in the coast of Kent.
How comes it then that such a knave as you
Dare swear a matter of such consequence?

GREENE

Ah, Will—   145

BLACK WILL

Tush, give me leave, there's no more but this:
Sith thou hast sworn, we dare discover all,

---

125 *Go to* exclamation of protest   137 *known* Q2–3 (kowne Q1)
130 *urge* bring up   147 *Sith* since
135 speech heading Q2–3 (not in Q1)   *discover* reveal

And hadst thou or shouldst thou utter it,
We have devised a complot under hand,
Whatever shall betide to any of us,   150
To send thee roundly to the devil of hell.
And therefore thus: I am the very man,
Marked in my birth-hour by the Destinies,
To give an end to Arden's life on earth;
Thou but a member but to whet the knife   155
Whose edge must search the closet of his breast.
Thy office is but to appoint the place,
And train thy master to his tragedy;
Mine to perform it when occasion serves.
Then be not nice, but here devise with us   160
How and what way we may conclude his death.

SHAKEBAG
So shalt thou purchase Mosby for thy friend,
And by his friendship gain his sister's love.
GREENE
So shall thy mistress be thy favourer,
And thou disburdened of the oath thou made.   165
MICHAEL
Well, gentlemen, I cannot but confess,
Sith you have urged me so apparently,
That I have vowed my master Arden's death;
And he whose kindly love and liberal hand
Doth challenge nought but good deserts of me   170
I will deliver over to your hands.
This night come to his house at Aldersgate;
The doors I'll leave unlocked against you come.

149 *complot* Q2–3 (complat Q1) plot, conspiracy
   under hand in secret
151 *roundly* promptly, directly
155 *member* helper
158 *train* lure
160 *nice* coy, squeamish
170 *challenge* claim, deserve
   deserts of deeds in return from
173 *against you come* in anticipation of your coming

153 *Destinies* i.e., the three Goddesses of Fate.

No sooner shall ye enter through the latch,
Over the threshold to the inner court,   175
But on your left hand shall you see the stairs
That leads directly to my master's chamber.
There take him and dispose him as ye please.
Now it were good we parted company.
What I have promised I will perform.   180

BLACK WILL
Should you deceive us, 'twould go wrong with you.

MICHAEL
I will accomplish all I have revealed.

BLACK WILL
Come, let's go drink. Choler makes me as dry as a dog.

Exeunt [BLACK] WILL, GREENE, and
SHAKEBAG. *Manet* MICHAEL

MICHAEL
Thus feeds the lamb securely on the down
Whilst through the thicket of an arbour brake   185
The hunger-bitten wolf o'erpries his haunt
And takes advantage to eat him up.
Ah, harmless Arden, how, how hast thou misdone
That thus thy gentle life is levelled at?
The many good turns that thou hast done to me   190
Now must I quittance with betraying thee.
I, that should take the weapon in my hand
And buckler thee from ill-intending foes,
Do lead thee with a wicked, fraudful smile,
As unsuspected to the slaughterhouse.   195
So have I sworn to Mosby and my mistress,
So have I promised to the slaughtermen;
And should I not deal currently with them,
Their lawless rage would take revenge on me.
Tush, I will spurn at mercy for this once.   200
Let pity lodge where feeble women lie;
I am resolved, and Arden needs must die.

Exit MICHAEL

183 s.d. *Manet* remains
186 *haunt* ed. (hant Qq)
188 *harmless* innocent
189 *levelled at* aimed at, threatened
191 *quittance* repay
193 *buckler,* shield, protect
198 *currently* honestly, faithfully

Scene IV

Here enters ARDEN *and* FRANKLIN

ARDEN

No, Franklin, no. If fear or stormy threats,
If love of me or care of womanhood,
If fear of God or common speech of men,
Who mangle credit with their wounding words
And couch dishonour as dishonour buds,   5
Might 'join repentance in her wanton thoughts,
No question then but she would turn the leaf
And sorrow for her dissolution.
But she is rooted in her wickedness,
Perverse and stubborn, not to be reclaimed.   10
Good counsel is to her as rain to weeds,
And reprehension makes her vice to grow
As Hydra's head that plenished by decay.

4 *credit* honour, reputation	8 *dissolution* dissolute behaviour
6 *'join* enjoin	13 *plenished* ed. (perisht Qq) replenished

1–10 See Intro., p. xxi

  5 *couch* a difficult word, glossed differently by various editors. Warnke and Proescholdt (*Pseudo-Shakesperian Plays*, Vol. V), suggest *spread*, comparing *couch grass;* R. Bayne notes that if the word is used 'in its surgical sense' ('to remove a cataract' *O.E.D.* 9), the line would mean 'Cut the bud of dishonour so tht it bursts into flower.' Sturgess glosses it as 'to embroider' (*O.E.D.* †4b), and Wine suggests that a 'possible, but more remote, reading might be based on *O.E.D.* 15 ('to put into words'). Brooke's suggestion (based on *O.E.D.* v¹., 5 'to promote germination'), that the line 'appears to mean that scandal mongers nourish the unripe buds of dishonour, as fast as they appear, till they sprout and grow', has the advantage of keeping to the imagery of the speech and to a pattern of imagery running through the whole play. According to *O.E.D.*, however, this usage refers specifically to *'Malting*. To lay or spread (grain after steeping) on a floor to promote germination'. Although that may be apt for a play set in Kent, a more specific, and equally appropriate horticultural gloss (*O.E.D.* 3†c, 'to lay, set, bed (plants or slips) in the earth'), would give the reading: 'As the buds (or shoots) of dishonour appear, so the scandal mongers plant them in the earth (or *couch* them) to grow stronger', a reading supported, perhaps, by 1.9, 'But she is rooted in her wickedness'.
    Interestingly (in view of 1.13), the *O.E.D.* entry for *bud* (3.fig.), cites the example 'This Hydra. . . With seven heads, budding monstrous crimes' (1591).

13 The second labour of Hercules was to kill the Lernaean Hydra, an enormous serpent with nine heads, each of which was *replenished* with two more when cut off; (*by decay* = ?by decapitation—Wine).

Her faults, methink, are painted in my face
For every searching eye to overread;   15
And Mosby's name, a scandal unto mine,
Is deeply trenched in my blushing brow.
Ah, Franklin, Franklin, when I think on this,
My heart's grief rends my other powers
Worse than the conflict at the hour of death.   20

FRANKLIN
Gentle Arden, leave this sad lament.
She will amend, and so your griefs will cease;
Or else she'll die, and so your sorrows end.
If neither of these two do haply fall,
Yet let your comfort be that others bear   25
Your woes, twice doubled all, with patience.

insight perceived into women's faults

ARDEN
My house is irksome; there I cannot rest.

FRANKLIN
Then stay with me in London; go not home.

ARDEN
Then that base Mosby doth usurp my room
And makes his triumph of my being thence.   30
At home or not at home, where'er I be,
Here, here it lies, [*points to his heart*] ah, Franklin, here it lies
That will not out till wretched Arden dies.

Here enters MICHAEL

FRANKLIN
Forget your griefs awhile; here comes your man.

ARDEN
What o'clock is't, sirrah?

MICHAEL   Almost ten.   35

ARDEN
See, see how runs away the weary time.
Come, Master Franklin, shall we go to bed?

Exeunt ARDEN *and* MICHAEL
Manet FRANKLIN

FRANKLIN
I pray you, go before; I'll follow you.
Ah, what a hell is fretful jealousy!
What pity-moving words, what deep-fetched sighs,   40

17 *trenched* furrowed, carved
24 *fall* occur
40 *moving* Q2–3 (moning Q1)

What grievous groans and overlading woes
Accompanies this gentle gentleman.
Now will he shake his care-oppressed head,
Then fix his sad eyes on the sullen earth,
Ashamed to gaze upon the open world;   45
Now will he cast his eyes up towards the heavens,
Looking that ways for redress of wrong.
Sometimes he seeketh to beguile his grief,
And tells a story with his careful tongue;
Then comes his wife's dishonour in his thoughts   50
And in the middle cutteth off his tale,
Pouring fresh sorrow on his weary limbs.
So woe-begone, so inly charged with woe,
Was never any lived and bare it so.

Here enters MICHAEL

MICHAEL
My master would desire you come to bed.   55
FRANKLIN
Is he himself already in his bed?

Exit FRANKLIN. *Manet* MICHAEL

MICHAEL
He is and fain would have the light away.
Conflicting thoughts encamped in my breast
Awake me with the echo of their strokes;
And I, a judge to censure either side,   60
Can give to neither wished victory.
My master's kindness pleads to me for life
With just demand, and I must grant it him;
My mistress she hath forced me with an oath,

48 *beguile* divert attention away from
49 *careful* full of care
54 *Was* i.e. there was
60 *censure* pronounce judgement on

58–86 This impressive soliloquy which (like Mosby's at the opening of Scene VIII), strikingly reveals the conflicting emotions within the character is not found in Holinshed's narrative, though Wine (p. xli) suggests that the playwright might have been inspired by the marginal gloss added to the second edition of the *Chronicles,* 'Note here the force of feare and a troubled conscience', observing that although 'Holinshed in several places points out Michael's fear of Black Will . . . the chronicler never endows him with even a suggestion of the "troubled conscience" '

For Susan's sake the which I may not break,   65
For that is nearer than a master's love;
That grim-faced fellow, pitiless Black Will,
And Shakebag, stern in bloody stratagem—
Two rougher ruffians never lived in Kent—
Have sworn my death if I infringe my vow,   70
A dreadful thing to be considered of.
Methinks I see them with their boltered hair,
Staring and grinning in thy gentle face,
And in their ruthless hands their daggers drawn,
Insulting o'er thee with a peck of oaths   75
Whilst thou, submissive, pleading for relief,
Art mangled by their ireful instruments.
Methinks I hear them ask where Michael is,
And pitiless Black Will cries 'Stab the slave!
The peasant will detect the tragedy.'   80
The wrinkles in his foul, death-threat'ning face
Gapes open wide, like graves to swallow men.
My death to him is but a merriment,
And he will murder me to make him sport.
He comes, he comes! Ah, Master Franklin, help!   85
Call up the neighbours or we are but dead.
                    Here enters FRANKLIN *and* ARDEN
FRANKLIN
What dismal outcry calls me from my rest?
ARDEN
What hath occasioned such a fearful cry?
Speak, Michael! Hath any injured thee?
MICHAEL
Nothing, sir; but as I fell asleep   90
Upon the threshold, leaning to the stairs,
I had a fearful dream that troubled me,
And in my slumber thought I was beset
With murderer thieves that came to rifle me.
My trembling joints witness my inward fear.   95
I crave your pardons for disturbing you.
ARDEN
So great a cry for nothing I ne'er heard.
What, are the doors fast locked and all things safe?

75 *Insulting* exulting	80 *detect* reveal, disclose
thee Q3 (there Q1–2)	91 *leaning to* leaning against
peck heap	94 *rifle* rob

72 *boltered* ed. (bolstred Qq) in tangled knots, or matted with congealed blood (cf. *Macbeth*, IV.i, 123, 'blood-bolter'd Banquo').

MICHAEL

I cannot tell; I think I locked the doors.

ARDEN

I like not this, but I'll go see myself.   [*He tries the doors*]   100
Ne'er trust me but the doors were all unlocked.
This negligence not half contenteth me.
Get you to bed, and if you love my favour
Let me have no more such pranks as these.
Come, Master Franklin, let us go to bed.   105

FRANKLIN

Ay, by my faith; the air is very cold.
Michael, farewell; I pray thee dream no more.   *Exeunt*

Scene V

Here enters [BLACK] WILL, GREENE, *and* SHAKEBAG

SHAKEBAG

Black night hath hid the pleasures of the day,
And sheeting darkness overhangs the earth
And with the black fold of her cloudy robe
Obscures us from the eyesight of the world,
In which sweet silence such as we triumph.   5
The lazy minutes linger on their time,
Loth to give due audit to the hour,
Till in the watch our purpose be complete,
And Arden sent to everlasting night.
Greene, get you gone and linger here about,   10
And at some hour hence come to us again,
Where we will give you instance of his death.

GREENE

Speed to my wish whose will so'er says no;
And so I'll leave you for an hour or two.   *Exit* GREENE

106 *by* Q2–3 (be Q1)
107 s.d. So Q2–3. After l.106 in Q1

s.d. So Q2–3; after l.1 in Q1   12 *instance* evidence
  2 *sheeting* enfolding, covering   13 *speed* success

---

100 s.d. Presumably Arden moves to the doors at the back of the stage.

1–5 These lines may perhaps seem strange coming from Shakebag, but the
  playwright's primary concern here is to establish the *mood* of this night scene as
  effectively as possible.
8 *watch* one of the periods into which the night was divided.

BLACK WILL

    I tell thee, Shakebag, would this thing were done;   15
    I am so heavy that I can scarce go.
    This drowsiness in me bodes little good.

SHAKEBAG

    How now, Will, become a precisian?
    Nay, then, let's go sleep when bugs and fears
    Shall kill our courages with their fancy's work.   20

BLACK WILL

    Why, Shakebag, thou mistakes me much ·
    And wrongs me too in telling me of fear.
    Wert not a serious thing we go about,
    It should be slipped till I had fought with thee
    To let thee know I am no coward, I.   25
    I tell thee, Shakebag, thou abusest me.

SHAKEBAG

    Why, thy speech bewrayed an inly kind of fear,
    And savoured of a weak, relenting spirit.
    Go forward now in that we have begun,
    And afterwards attempt me when thou darest.   30

BLACK WILL

    And if I do not, heaven cut me off!
    But let that pass, and show me to this house,
    Where thou shalt see I'll do as much as Shakebag.

SHAKEBAG

    This is the door [*He tries it*]—but soft, methinks 'tis shut.
    The villain Michael hath deceived us.   35

BLACK WILL

    Soft, let me see. Shakebag, 'tis shut indeed.
    Knock with thy sword; perhaps the slave will hear.

---

18 *precisian* puritan
19 *bugs* bugbears, imaginary terrors
20 *fancy's* ed. (fancies Qq)
    fancy's work effect on our imaginations
22 *telling* accusing
24 *slipped* put off
27 *bewrayed* revealed, betrayed
30 *attempt* try your luck with, engage

---

34 *the door* as in the previous scene (1. 100) one of the doors at the back of the stage,
    though now imagined seen from the outside. The change from interior to
    exterior scene is thereby easily defined.

SHAKEBAG
  It will not be; the white-livered peasant
  Is gone to bed and laughs us both to scorn.
BLACK WILL
  And he shall buy his merriment as dear   40
  As ever coistrel bought so little sport.
  Ne'er let this sword assist me when I need,
  But rust and canker after I have sworn,
  If I, the next time that I meet the hind,
  Lop not away his leg, his arm, or both.   45
SHAKEBAG
  And let me never draw a sword again,
  Nor prosper in the twilight, cockshut light,
  When I would fleece the wealthy passenger,
  But lie and languish in a loathsome den,
  Hated and spit at by the goers-by,   50
  And in that death may die unpitied
  If I, the next time that I meet the slave,
  Cut not the nose from off the coward's face
  And trample on it for this villainy.
BLACK WILL
  Come, let's go seek out Greene; I know he'll swear.   55
SHAKEBAG
  He were a villain and he would not swear.
  'Twould make a peasant swear amongst his boys,
  That ne'er durst say before but 'yea' and 'no',
  To be thus flouted of a coisterel.
BLACK WILL
  Shakebag, let's seek out Greene, and in the morning,   60
  At the alehouse 'butting Arden's house,
  Watch the out-coming of that prick-eared cur,
  And then let me alone to handle him.   *Exeunt*

41 *coistrel* knave (see l.59 for variant spelling)
44 *hind* fellow, servant
48 *passenger* traveller on foot
62 *prick-eared* having pointed ears

---

38 *white-livered* cowardly. Cf. 'the liver white and pale, which is the badge of
   pusillanimity and cowardice' (*2 Henry IV*, IV.iii, 103–4).
47 *cockshut light* 'the close of the evening at which time poultry go to roost'
   (Johnson). Florio's defintion (*A Worlde of Wordes*, London, 1598), 'when a man
   cannot discerne a dog from a wolfe' is exactly in keeping with the mood of the
   speech and scene.
57 Sturgess considers the line 'feeble', and is 'tempted to read "pedant"
   (=schoolteacher) for "peasant".' (Qq read *pesant*.)

Scene VI

Here enters ARDEN, FRANKLIN, *and* MICHAEL

ARDEN
  Sirrah, get you back to Billingsgate
  And learn what time the tide will serve our turn.
  Come to us in Paul's. First go make the bed,
  And afterwards go hearken for the flood.   *Exit* MICHAEL
  Come, Master Franklin, you shall go with me.   5
  This night I dreamed that being in a park,
  A toil was pitched to overthrow the deer,
  And I upon a little rising hill
  Stood whistly watching for the herd's approach.
  Even there, methoughts, a gentle slumber took me,   10
  And summoned all my parts to sweet repose.
  But in the pleasure of this golden rest
  An ill-thewed foster had removed the toil,
  And rounded me with that beguiling home
  Which late, methought, was pitched to cast the deer.   15
  With that he blew an evil-sounding horn,
  And at the noise another herdman came
  With falchion drawn, and bent it at my breast,
  Crying aloud, 'Thou art the game we seek.'

  7 *toil* net
  9 *whistly* silently
13 *ill-thewed* ill-natured
   foster forester
14 *rounded . . .home* trapped me with the net
15 *cast* overthrow
18 *bent* aimed

  1 *Billingsgate* 'The principal of the old water-gates of London, on the north side of
  the Thames, east of London Bridge. . . . It was a usual landing place for
  travellers from abroad or from the lower reaches of the Thames' (Sugden).

18 *falchion* (fauchon Qq) a curved broad-sword with the edge on the convex side (cf.
  Richard III, I.ii, 94–5, 'Thy murd'rous falchion smoking in his blood;/The
  which thou once didst bend against her breast').

With this I waked and trembled every joint,   20
Like one obscured in a little bush
That sees a lion foraging about,
And when the dreadful forest king is gone,
He pries about with timorous suspect
Throughout the thorny casements of the brake,   25
And will not think his person dangerless,
But quakes and shivers though the cause be gone.
So trust me, Franklin, when I did awake
I stood in doubt whether I waked or no,
Such great impression took this fond surprise.   30
God grant this vision bedeem me any good.

FRANKLIN

This fantasy doth rise from Michael's fear,
Who being awaked with the noise he made,
His troubled senses yet could take no rest;
And this, I warrant you, procured your dream.   35

ARDEN

It may be so; God frame it to the best!
But oftentimes my dreams presage too true.

FRANKLIN

To such as note their nightly fantasies,
Some one in twenty may incur belief.
But use it not; 'tis but a mockery.   40

ARDEN

Come, Master Franklin, we'll now walk in Paul's,
And dine together at the ordinary,
And by my man's direction draw to the quay

---

24 *suspect* apprehension
27 *shivers* Q3 (shewers Q1−2)
30 *took . . .surprise* this foolish terror made upon me
31 *bedeem . . .good* fortells no danger for me
36 *frame* bring to pass
40 *use it not* do not engage in such a practice

---

25 *brake* thicket. *O.E.D.* (sb. 6I.) notes that the word can also mean 'trap or snare'.
32−5 Cf. Arden himself to Alice in Scene I (l. 74), 'there is no credit in a dream.'
43 *quay* the wharf at Billingsgate. From there Arden and Franklin would take the barge that plied daily between Billingsgate and Gravesend. The fare was twopence.

And with the tide go down to Faversham.
Say, Master Franklin, shall it not be so?   45
FRANKLIN
At your good pleasure, sir; I'll bear you company

Exeunt

Scene VII

Here enters MICHAEL *at one door. Here enters*
GREENE, [BLACK] WILL, *and* SHAKEBAG *at another door*

BLACK WILL
Draw, Shakebag, for here's that villain Michael.
GREENE
First, Will, let's hear what he can say.
BLACK WILL
Speak, milksop slave, and never after speak!
MICHAEL
For God's sake, sirs, let me excuse myself,
For here I swear by heaven and earth and all,   5
I did perform the outmost of my task,
And left the doors unbolted and unlocked.
But see the chance: Franklin and my master
Were very late conferring in the porch,
And Franklin left his napkin where he sat,   10
With certain gold knit in it, as he said.
Being in bed he did bethink himself,
And coming down he found the doors unshut.
He locked the gates and brought away the keys,
For which offence my master rated me.   15
But now I am going to see what flood it is,
For with the tide my master will away,
Where you may front him well on Rainham Down,
A place well-fitting such a stratagem.

3 *milksop* cowardly	11 *knit* tied up
6 *outmost* utmost	15 *rated* berated
8 *chance* mischance	18 *front* Q3 (frons Q1–2) confront
10 *napkin* handkerchief	

---

18 *Rainham Down* the open countryside around Rainham, a village in Kent, about
  5 miles from Rochester on the road to Faversham. 'The road from Gravesend to
  Dover was infested by tramps, highwaymen, and ruffians of every sort, and the
  solitary traveller can never have been safe . . .Exposed places like Gad's Hill
  and Rainham Down were notoriously dangerous' (Cust, p. 125).

BLACK WILL

    Your excuse hath somewhat mollified my choler.   20
    Why now, Greene, 'tis better now nor e'er it was.

GREENE

    But, Michael, is this true?

MICHAEL

    As true as I report it to be true.

SHAKEBAG

    Then, Michael, this shall be your penance:
    To feast us all at the Salutation,   25
    Where we will plot our purpose thoroughly.

GREENE

    And, Michael, you shall bear no news of this tide
    Because they two may be in Rainham Down
    Before your master.

MICHAEL

    Why, I'll agree to anything you'll have me,   30
    So you will except of my company.   *Exeunt*

Scene VIII

Here enters MOSBY

MOSBY

    Disturbed thoughts drives me from company
    And dries my marrow with their watchfulness.
    Continual trouble of my moody brain
    Feebles my body by excess of drink
    And nips me as the bitter north-east wind   5
    Doth check the tender blossoms in the spring.
    Well fares the man, howe'er his cates do taste,

21 *nor* than
26 *plot* ed. (plat Qq)
31 *except* Q1–2 (accept Q3)
  7 *cates* delicacies, choice food

---

25 *Salutation* a tavern in Newgate Street. 'The sign probably represented the meeting between Gabriel and the Virgin Mary' (Sugden).

31 *except* Q1–2. (accept Q3). Either reading is possible. Q1–2 reading is supported by Michael's wish (III, 179) not to be seen in the cut-throats' company. The attempt on Arden's life in Scene V failed, however, only because Michael did not perform all he had promised, and now he might be more likely to want to ingratiate himself with the murderers. *O.E.D.* cites an example (1635) of *except* used mistakenly for *accept* which might lend further support to Q3's reading.

That tables not with foul suspicion;
And he but pines amongst his delicates
Whose troubled mind is stuffed with discontent.   10
My golden time was when I had no gold.
Though then I wanted, yet I slept secure;
My daily toil begat me night's repose,
My night's repose made daylight fresh to me.
But since I climbed the top bough of the tree   15
And sought to build my nest among the clouds,
Each gentlest airy gale doth shake my bed
And makes me dread my downfall to the earth.
But whither doth contemplation carry me?
The way I seek to find, where pleasure dwells,   20
Is hedged behind me that I cannot back
But needs must on although to danger's gate.
Then, Arden, perish thou by that decree,
For Greene doth ear the land and weed thee up
To make my harvest nothing but pure corn.   25
And for his pains I'll heave him up awhile
And, after, smother him to have his wax;

8 *tables* dines
12 *Though* Q2–3 (Thought Q1)
17 *gentlest airy gale* ed. (gentle stary gaile Qq)
24 *ear* plough
26 *heave him up* extol him

9 *delicates* usually glossed as 'delicacies' or 'choice food', but *O.E.D.* IV.B.2†a., 'luxuries, delights' is possibly more appropriate, as Mosby develops the sense of his life of material well-being.

17 *Each gentlest airy gale* ed. (Each gentle stary gaile Qq) This emendation (also accepted by Sturgess) was proposed by P. A. McElwaine in *'Arden of Feversham'*, *N. & Q.* 11th ser., II (1910), p. 226, on the grounds that "Each gentlest" is not un-Elizabethan, and whether the *i* in "gaile" is a compositor's misplacement of the *i* in "airy" or not, would not much matter. A loose orthography might spell "airy" as "ary" . . . ."Gale" . . . just means a zephyr. "Airy" would emphasize the gentleness of the gale which disturbs one "Whose troubled mind is stuffed with discontent".'
Wine emends to *starry* (first proposed by Jacob) but I am not as convinced as he is by R. D. Cornelius's explanation of how a 'gale blowing among the stars' is an appropriate image for Mosby to use (see 'Mosbie's "Stary Gaile"', *Philological Quarterly*, IX, 1930, p. 72).

27 *smother . . .wax* refers to the practice of smoking out bees in order to obtain the wax and honey from the hive.

Such bees as Greene must never live to sting.
Then is there Michael and the painter too,
Chief actors to Arden's overthrow,   30
Who, when they shall see me sit in Arden's seat,
They will insult upon me for my meed,
Or fright me by detecting of his end.
I'll none of that, for I can cast a bone
To make these curs pluck out each other's throat,   35
And then am I sole ruler of mine own.
Yet Mistress Arden lives; but she's myself,
And holy church rites make us two but one.
But what for that I may not trust you, Alice?
You have supplanted Arden for my sake,   40
And will extirpen me to plant another.
'Tis fearful sleeping in a serpent's bed,
And I will cleanly rid my hands of her.
            Here enters ALICE [*with a prayerbook*]
But here she comes, and I must flatter her.
How now, Alice! What, sad and passionate?   45
Make me partaker of thy pensiveness;
Fire divided burns with lesser force.

ALICE
But I will dam that fire in my breast
Till by the force thereof my part consume.
Ah, Mosby!   50

MOSBY
Such deep pathaires, like to a cannon's burst
Discharged against a ruinated wall,

---

32 *meed* reward
41 *extirpen* root out, destroy
45 *passionate* sorrowful
52 *ruinated* ruined

---

34 *a bone* i.e., Susan.
37–8 According to Holinshed, Alice and Mosby had promised 'to be in all points
    as man and wife togither, and therevpon they both receiued the sacrament on a
    sundaie at London, openlie in a church there.' The playwright makes no
    specific reference to this event, though Arden refers (I, 17–18) to Mosby
    wearing the ring 'Which at our marriage day the priest put on', and Mosby
    twice refers to himself as Alice's 'husband' (I, 638 and XIV, 273) in Alice's
    presence.
48–9 'I will suppress the passion that I have for you until by force of its own
    violence it consumes itself and disappears' (Wine). Cf. I, 207–8.

Breaks my relenting heart in thousand pieces.
Ungentle Alice, thy sorrow is my sore;
Thou know'st it well, and 'tis thy policy   55
To forge distressful looks to wound a breast
Where lies a heart that dies when thou art sad.
It is not love that loves to anger love.

ALICE
It is not love that loves to murder love.

MOSBY
How mean you that?   60

ALICE
Thou knowest how dearly Arden loved me.

MOSBY
And then?

ALICE
And then—conceal the rest, for 'tis too bad,
Lest that my words be carried with the wind
And published in the world to both our shames.   65
I pray thee, Mosby, let our springtime wither;
Our harvest else will yield but loathsome weeds.
Forget, I pray thee, what hath passed betwixt us,
For now I blush and tremble at the thoughts.

MOSBY
What, are you changed?   70

ALICE
Ay, to my former happy life again;
From title of an odious strumpet's name
To honest Arden's wife—not Arden's honest wife.
Ha, Mosby, 'tis thou hast rifled me of that,
And made me sland'rous to all my kin.   75
Even in my forehead is thy name engraven,
A mean artificer, that low-born name.
I was bewitched; woe worth the hapless hour

---

57 *when* Q2–3 (where Q1)
78 *woe worth* a curse upon
   hapless unfortunate

---

51 *pathaires* sad and passionate outbursts. The word does not appear in the *O.E.D.*,
   but P. Simpson (*Modern Language Review*, I, 1906 , pp. 326–7), has proved its
   authenticity, citing another usage in W. Smith's *The Hector of Germanie*, 1615.
73 *honest* 2 chaste. The second part of the line is clearly in response to, or
   anticipation of, Mosby's reaction to her change of heart.

And all the causes that enchanted me!
MOSBY
Nay, if thou ban, let me breathe curses forth,   80
And, if you stand so nicely at your fame,
Let me repent the credit I have lost.
I have neglected matters of import
That would have stated me above thy state,
Forslowed advantages, and spurned at time.   85
Ay, Fortune's right hand Mosby hath forsook
To take a wanton giglot by the left.
I left the marriage of an honest maid
Whose dowry would have weighed down all thy wealth,
Whose beauty and demeanour far exceeded thee.   90
This certain good I lost for changing bad,
And wrapped my credit in thy company.
I was bewitched—that is no theme of thine!—
And thou unhallowed hast enchanted me.
But I will break thy spells and exorcisms,   95
And put another sight upon these eyes
That showed my heart a raven for a dove.
Thou art not fair, I viewed thee not till now;
Thou art not kind, till now I knew thee not.
And now the rain hath beaten off thy gilt   100
Thy worthless copper shows thee counterfeit.
It grieves me not to see how foul thou art,
But mads me that ever I thought thee fair.
Go, get thee gone, a copesmate for thy hinds!
I am too good to be thy favourite.   105
ALICE
Ay, now I see, and too soon find it true,
Which often hath been told me by my friends,
That Mosby loves me not but for my wealth,

80 *ban* curse
81 *stand so nicely at* insist so fastidiously on
   fame honour, reputation
84 *stated . . .state* raised me above your rank
85 *Forslowed* wasted
87 *giglot* lewd, worthless woman
94 *unhallowed* wicked
95 *exorcisms* spells
104 *copesmate* companion (in contemptuous sense)

92 *wrapped my credit in thy company* see Intro., p. xxvii

Which too incredulous I ne'er believed.
Nay, hear me speak, Mosby, a word or two;   110
I'll bite my tongue if it speak bitterly.
Look on me, Mosby, or I'll kill myself;
Nothing shall hide me from thy stormy look.
If thou cry war there is no peace for me.
I will do penance for offending thee   115
And burn this prayerbook, where I here use
The holy word that had converted me.
See, Mosby, I will tear away the leaves,
And all the leaves, and in this golden cover
Shall thy sweet phrases and thy letters dwell,   120
And thereon will I chiefly meditate
And hold no other sect but such devotion.
Wilt thou not look? Is all thy love o'erwhelmed?
Wilt thou not hear? What malice stops thine ears?
Why speaks thou not? What silence ties thy tongue?   125
Thou hast been sighted as the eagle is,
And heard as quickly as the fearful hare,
And spoke as smoothly as an orator,
When I have bid thee hear, or see, or speak.
And art thou sensible in none of these?   130
Weigh all thy good turns with this little fault
And I deserve not Mosby's muddy looks.
A fount once troubled is not thickened still;
Be clear again, I'll ne'er more trouble thee.

---

116 *where* wherein
122 *hold . . .sect* keep no other religious faith
127 *quickly* keenly, sharply
130 *sensible* capable of feeling, expressing, or perceiving
133 *fount once troubled* ed. (fence of trouble Qq)
    still for ever

109–110 Alice's change of direction in the speech is so abrupt that it must be prompted by some definite action on Mosby's part: perhaps he goes to leave.
131 *thy . . .turns* i.e., all the good turns I've done for you.
133 *A fount once troubled* ed. (A fence of trouble Qq) This emendation was proposed by W. Headlam in *The Athanaeum*, 26 December 1903, who argued that 'the text arose from writing or printing "A fonce troubled" instead of "A fon[t on]ce troubled"'. M.P. Jackson (p.50), cites a Shakespearean parallel (*Troilus and Cressida*, III.iii, 310–11): 'My mind is troubled, like a fountain stirred, And I myself not see the bottom of it.'

MOSBY

Oh, no, I am a base artificer,   135
My wings are feathered for a lowly flight.
Mosby? Fie, no! not for a thousand pound.
Make love to you? Why, 'tis unpardonable;
We beggars must not breathe where gentles are.

ALICE

Sweet Mosby is as gentle as a king,   140
And I too blind to judge him otherwise.
Flowers do sometimes spring in fallow lands,
Weeds in gardens, roses grow on thorns;
So whatso'er my Mosby's father was,
Himself is valued gentle by his worth.   145

MOSBY

Ah, how you women can insinuate,
And clear a trespass with your sweet-set tongue.
I will forget this quarrel, gentle Alice,
Provided I'll be tempted so no more.
                    Here enters BRADSHAW

ALICE

Then with thy lips seal up this new-made match.   150

MOSBY

Soft, Alice, for here comes somebody.

ALICE

How now, Bradshaw, what's the news with you?

BRADSHAW

I have little news, but here's a letter
That Master Greene importuned me to give you.

ALICE

Go in, Bradshaw; call for a cup of beer.   155
'Tis almost suppertime; thou shalt stay with us.
                              Exit [BRADSHAW]
                 Then she reads the letter
'We have missed of our purpose at London, but shall
perform it by the way. We thank our neighbour Bradshaw.
                         Yours, Richard Greene.'

139 *gentles* of gentle birth or rank   147 *clear a trespass* acquit (yourselves)
140 *gentle* noble   156 s.d. Q2–3; after l. 155 Q1.
145 *is* ed. (not in Qq)

---

157 The letter was written, of course, in Scene II (while Bradshaw was asking Black
    Will for information), and before the failed attempts on Arden's life in Scenes
    III and V.

How likes my love the tenor of this letter?   160
MOSBY
Well, were his date complete and expired.
ALICE
Ah, would it were! Then comes my happy hour.
Till then my bliss is mixed with bitter gall.
Come, let us in to shun suspicion.
MOSBY
Ay, to the gates of death to follow thee.   *Exeunt* 165

Scene IX

Here enters GREENE, [BLACK] WILL, *and* SHAKEBAG

SHAKEBAG
Come, Will, see thy tools be in a readiness.
Is not thy powder dank, or will thy flint strike fire?
BLACK WILL
Then ask me if my nose be on my face,
Or whether my tongue be frozen in my mouth.
Zounds, here's a coil!   5
You were best swear me on the intergatories
How many pistols I have took in hand,
Or whether I love the smell of gunpowder,
Or dare abide the noise the dag will make,
Or will not wink at flashing of the fire.   10
I pray thee, Shakebag, let this answer thee,
That I have took more purses in this Down
Than e'er thou handlest pistols in thy life.
SHAKEBAG
Ay, haply thou hast picked more in a throng;
But should I brag what booties I have took,   15
I think the overplus that's more than thine
Would mount to a greater sum of money
Than either thou or all thy kin are worth.
Zounds, I hate them as I hate a toad
That carry a muscado in their tongue   20
And scarce a hurting weapon in their hand

5 *coil* fuss
6 *intergatories* syncopated form of *interrogatories:* questions 'formally put to an accused person or witness' (*O.E.D.*)
9 *dag* pistol
10 *wink* blink
20 *muscado* ?musket

BLACK WILL
  Oh Greene, intolerable!
  It is not for mine honour to bear this.
  Why, Shakebag, I did serve the king at Boulogne,
  And thou canst brag of nothing that thou has done.   25
SHAKEBAG
  Why, so can Jack of Faversham,
  That sounded for a fillip on the nose,
  When he that gave it him holloed in his ear,
  And he supposed a cannon-bullet hit him.
                    Then they fight

GREENE
  I pray you, sirs, list to Aesop's talk: 30
  Whilst two stout dogs were striving for a bone,
  There comes a cur and stole it from them both;
  So, while you stand striving on these terms of manhood,
  Arden escapes us and deceives us all.
SHAKEBAG
  Why, he begun.
BLACK WILL   And thou shalt find I'll end.   35
  I do but slip it until better time.
  But if I do forget—
      Then he kneels down and holds up his hands to heaven
GREENE
  Well, take your fittest standings, and once more
  Lime your twigs to catch this weary bird.
  I'll leave you, and at your dag's discharge   40
  Make towards, like the longing water-dog
  That coucheth till the fowling-piece be off,

---

27 *sounded* swooned, fainted	31 *stout* valiant
fillip sharp blow with the fist	42 *coucheth* lies down
28 *holloed* bellowed	

30 *Aesop's talk* References to the fables of Aesop (a Greek slave who is supposed to
  have lived in the sixth century B.C.), are common in Elizabethan drama. See also
  VIII, 34–5.
38 *fittest standings* See III, 37n.
39 *lime . . .bird* Birdlime was a sticky substance spread (or limed) on branches to
  catch birds.
  weary wearisome or tedious (because it is taking much longer to kill Arden than
  Greene had anticipated).
42 *fowling piece* A light gun used for shooting wild fowl, which would be retrieved
  by the *water-dog.*

Then seizeth on the prey with eager mood.
Ah, might I see him stretching forth his limbs
As I have seen them beat their wings ere now.   45

SHAKEBAG

Why, that thou shalt see if he come this way.

GREENE

Yes, that he doth, Shakebag, I warrant thee.
But brawl not when I am gone in any case,
But, sirs, be sure to speed him when he comes;
And in that hope I'll leave you for an hour.   50

Exit GREENE
[BLACK WILL *and* SHAKEBAG *take up their positions*]
Here enters ARDEN, FRANKLIN, *and* MICHAEL

MICHAEL

'Twere best that I went back to Rochester.
The horse halts downright; it were not good
He travelled in such pain to Faversham.
Removing of a shoe may haply help it.

ARDEN

Well, get you back to Rochester; but, sirrah, see ye   55
Overtake us ere we come to Rainham Down,
For it will be very late ere we get home.

MICHAEL

[*Aside*] Ay, God he knows, and so doth Will and Shakebag,
That thou shalt never go further than that Down;
And therefore have I pricked the horse on purpose,   60
Because I would not view the massacre.   *Exit* MICHAEL

ARDEN

Come, Master Franklin, onwards with your tale.

FRANKLIN

I assure you, sir, you task me much.
A heavy blood is gathered at my heart,
And on the sudden is my wind so short   65

---

52 *halts downright* limps badly   64 *heavy* oppressive

---

45 *them* i.e., the waterfowl.
50 s.d. possibly behind one of the stage pillars.
56 Black Will and Shakebag, who are also on stage, are, of course, already at
Rainham Down. Arden and Franklin make their way there by walking round
the stage while Franklin tells his tale and Black Will and Shakebag remain
concealed. The murderers emerge as Arden and Franklin approach ('Stand
close, Will, I hear them coming') but are thwarted by the sudden appearance
through the rear doors of Lord Cheiny and his retinue, and by Lord Cheiny
evidently placing himself (unintentionally) between the murderers and Arden.
60 *pricked the horse* i.e., pierced the horse's foot to the quick, thereby laming it.

As hindereth the passage of my speech.
So fierce a qualm yet ne'er assailed me.

ARDEN

Come, Master Franklin, let us go on softly.
The annoyance of the dust or else some meat
You ate at dinner cannot brook with you.   70
I have been often so and soon amended.

FRANKLIN

Do you remember where my tale did leave?

ARDEN

Ay, where the gentleman did check his wife.

FRANKLIN

She being reprehended for the fact,
Witness produced that took her with the deed,   75
Her glove brought in which there she left behind,
And many other assured arguments,
Her husband asked her whether it were not so.

ARDEN

Her answer then? I wonder how she looked,
Having forsworn it with such vehement oaths,   80
And at the instant so approved upon her.

FRANKLIN

First did she cast her eyes down to the earth,
Watching the drops that fell amain from thence;
Then softly draws she forth her handkerchief,
And modestly she wipes her tear-stained face;   85
Then hemmed she out, to clear her voice should seem,
And with a majesty addressed herself
To encounter all their accusations.—
Pardon me, Master Arden, I can no more;
This fighting at my heart makes short my wind.   90

ARDEN

Come, we are almost now at Rainham Down.
Your pretty tale beguiles the weary way;
I would you were in state to tell it out.

67 *fierce* Q3 (ferse Q1–2)
68 *softly* gently, slowly
70 *brook with you* Q2–3 (brooke you Q1) agree with you
72 *leave* leave off
73 *check* reprimand, reprove
75 *took . . .deed* caught her in the act
77 *arguments* evidence
82 *approved upon* proved against
88 *encounter* counter, dispute

SHAKEBAG

[*Aside*] Stand close, Will, I hear them coming.

Here enters LORD CHEINY *with his* MEN

BLACK WILL

[*Aside*] Stand to it, Shakebag, and be resolute.   95

LORD CHEINY

Is it so near night as it seems,

Or will this black-faced evening have a shower?

[*Seeing* ARDEN] What, Master Arden? You are well met.

I have longed this fortnight's day to speak with you.

You are a stranger, man, in the Isle of Sheppey.   100

ARDEN

Your honour's always! Bound to do you service.

LORD CHEINY

Come you from London and ne'er a man with you?

ARDEN

My man's coming after,

But here's my honest friend that came along with me.

LORD CHEINY

[*To* FRANKLIN] My Lord Protector's man I take you to be.   105

FRANKLIN

Ay, my good lord, and highly bound to you.

LORD CHEINY

You and your friend come home and sup with me.

ARDEN

I beseech your honour pardon me;

I have made a promise to a gentleman,

My honest friend, to meet him at my house.   110

The occasion is great, or else would I wait on you.

LORD CHEINY

Will you come tomorrow and dine with me?

And bring your honest friend along with you.

I have divers matters to talk with you about.

ARDEN

Tomorrow we'll wait upon your honour.   115

LORD CHEINY

One of you stay my horse at the top of the hill.

[*Seeing* BLACK WILL]

What, Black Will! For whose purse wait you?

Thou wilt be hanged in Kent when all is done.

---

94 *Lord Cheiny* (1485?–1558); see Intro., p. xxiv

BLACK WILL
Not hanged, God save your honour.
I am your beadsman, bound to pray for you.   120
LORD CHEINY
I think thou ne'er saidest prayer in all thy life.
One of you give him a crown.
And, sirrah, leave this kind of life;
If thou beest 'tainted for a penny matter
And come in question, surely thou wilt truss.   125
Come, Master Arden, let us be going;
Your way and mine lies four mile together.   *Exeunt*
                              Manet BLACK WILL *and* SHAKEBAG

BLACK WILL
The Devil break all your necks at four miles' end!
Zounds, I could kill myself for very anger!
His lordship chops me in even when   130
My dag was levelled at his heart.
I would his crown were molten down his throat.
SHAKEBAG
Arden, thou hast wondrous ~~holy~~ luck.
Did ever man escape as thou hast done?
Well, I'll discharge my pistol at the sky,   135
For by this bullet Arden might not die.
                              Here enters GREENE

GREENE
What, is he down? Is he dispatched?
SHAKEBAG
Ay, in health towards Faversham to shame us all.
GREENE
The devil he is! Why, sirs, how escaped he?
SHAKEBAG
When we were ready to shoot   140
Comes my Lord Cheiny to prevent his death.

---

120 *beadsman* one paid to pray for others. Also used as a term to address superiors,
    cf. 'your humble servant'
125 *truss* hang
130 *chops me in* suddenly intervenes

124–5 'if you are accused of even the most trivial offence and are brought to trial,
    you'll hang for certain.'
131 *his* i.e., Arden's.
132 *his . . .his* i.e., Cheiny's.

GREENE

    The Lord of Heaven hath preserved him.

BLACK WILL

    The Lord of Heaven a fig! The Lord Cheiny hath preserved
       him,
    And bids him to a feast, to his house at Shorlow.
    But by the way once more I'll meet with him,   145
    And if all the Cheinies in the world say no,
    I'll have a bullet in his breast tomorrow.
    Therefore come, Greene, and let us to Faversham.

GREENE

    Ay, and excuse ourselves to Mistress Arden.
    Oh, how she'll chafe when she hears of this!   150

SHAKEBAG

    Why, I'll warrant you she'll think we dare not do it.

BLACK WILL

    Why then let us go and tell her all the matter,
    And plot the news to cut him off tomorrow.   *Exeunt*

Scene X

Here enters ARDEN *and his wife* [ALICE],
FRANKLIN *and* MICHAEL

ARDEN

    See how the Hours, the guardant of heaven's gate,
    Have by their toil removed the darksome clouds,
    That Sol may well discern the trampled pace

---

143 *The Lord of Heaven a fig!* ed. (Preserued, a figge, Qq)
153 *plot* Q3 (plat Q1 – 2)
    plot the news devise a new plan

 1 *guardant* keeper
 3 *Sol* the sun, personified
    discern Q2 – 3 (deserne; discerne); (deserue Q1)
    pace path

---

143 'Will's denial that Arden has been preserved ("Preserued, a figge") is
    contradictory. He should speak some such line as:
        The Lord of Heaven a fig! Lord Cheiny hath,
    the quibble being upon the two different kinds of "Lord"' (Jackson, p. 28).
144 *Shorlow* i.e., Shurland, Lord Cheiny's house on the Isle of Sheppey. (See map.)

 1 *the Hours* the daughters of Zeus and Themis, who were the custodians of the
    gates of Olympus, and who also governed changes in the weather.

Wherein he wont to guide his golden car.
The season fits; come, Franklin, let's away.   5

ALICE

I thought you did pretend some special hunt
That made you thus cut short the time of rest.

ARDEN

It was no chase that made me rise so early,
But, as I told thee yesternight, to go
To the Isle of Sheppey, there to dine with my Lord
    Cheiny,   10
For so his honour late commanded me.

ALICE

Ay, such kind husbands seldom want excuses.
Home is a wild cat to a wand'ring wit.
The time hath been — would God it were not past —
That honour's title nor a lord's command   15
Could once have drawn you from these arms of mine.
But my deserts or your desires decay,
Or both; yet if true love may seem desert,
I merit still to have thy company.

FRANKLIN

Why, I pray you, sir, let her go along with us;   20
I am sure his honour will welcome her,
And us the more for bringing her along.

ARDEN

Content. [*To* MICHAEL] Sirrah, saddle your mistress' nag.

ALICE

No. Begged favour merits little thanks.
If I should go our house would run away   25
Or else be stol'n; therefore I'll stay behind.

ARDEN

Nay, see how mistaking you are. I pray thee, go.

ALICE

No, no, not now.

ARDEN

Then let me leave thee satisfied in this:
That time nor place nor persons alter me,   30

11 *late* recently
12 *want* lack
17 *deserts* merits, good qualities
   desires ed. (deserues Q1; desernes Q2; deserves Q3)
18 *desert* deserving

6 *pretend* intend (though considering Alice's feelings towards Arden, the sub-text
of the word may well be 'to use as a pretext').

But that I hold thee dearer than my life.

ALICE

That will be seen by your quick return.

ARDEN

And that shall be ere night and if I live.

Farewell, sweet Alice; we mind to sup with thee.

                             Exit ALICE

FRANKLIN

Come, Michael, are our horses ready?   35

MICHAEL

Ay, your horses are ready, but I am not ready, for I have lost
my purse with six-and-thirty shillings in it, with taking up of
my master's nag.

FRANKLIN

Why, I pray you, let us go before,

Whilst he stays behind to seek his purse.   40

ARDEN

Go to, sirrah! See you follow us to the Isle of Sheppey,

To my Lord Cheiny's, where we mean to dine.

                  Exeunt ARDEN *and* FRANKLIN

                          Manet MICHAEL

MICHAEL

So, fair weather after you, for before you lies Black Will and
Shakebag in the broom close, too close for you. They'll be
your ferrymen to long home.   45

          Here enters the Painter [CLARKE]

But who is this? The painter, my co-rival, that would needs
win Mistress Susan.

CLARKE

How now, Michael? How doth my mistress and all at home?

---

33 *and if* if
37 *taking up* 'to bring (a horse, ox, etc.) from pasture into the stable or stall'
     (*O.E.D.*)
38 *master's* ed. (M. Q1 – 2; mistres Q3—see l.23 above)
44 *broom close* enclosed field of shrubs

---

45 *ferrymen* i.e., Charon, who conveyed the dead souls across the River Styx to
     Hades.
     to long home i.e., the grave. Cf. the proverb, 'He is gone to his long (last) home'
     (Tilley, H533). 'There is a quibble on "holme", meaning a little island in the
     river. Arden is about to take the ferry to the Isle of Sheppey; Michael says that
     the two murderers will act as his Charon-like ferrymen to a home/holme of a
     different kind' (Jackson, p. 175).

MICHAEL
Who? Susan Mosby? She is your mistress, too?

CLARKE
Ay. How doth she and all the rest?   50

MICHAEL
All's well but Susan; she is sick.

CLARKE
Sick? Of what disease?

MICHAEL
Of a great fear.

CLARKE
A fear of what?

MICHAEL
A great fever.   55

CLARKE
A fever! God forbid!

MICHAEL
Yes, faith, and of a lurdan, too, as big as yourself.

CLARKE
Oh, Michael, the spleen prickles you. Go to; you carry an
eye over Mistress Susan.

MICHAEL
Ay, faith, to keep her from the painter.   60

CLARKE
Why more from a painter than from a serving-creature like
yourself?

MICHAEL
Because you painters make but a painting-table of a pretty
wench and spoil her beauty with blotting.

CLARKE
What mean you by that?   65

---

58 *prickles* goads

---

57 *Lurdan* an insult meaning a rogue or loafer, and with a play on the term *fever-lurden,* the disease of laziness.

58 *spleen* an organ often associated with laughter, but also with heat, ill-temper, and irascibility, as it was believed to be the seat of melancholy and sudden passions.

58–9 *carry an eye over* have your eye on, fancy.

63 *painting-table* 'a board or other flat surface on which a picture is painted; hence, the picture itself' (*O.E.D., Table,* sb., †3).

64 *blotting* painting badly; but also with the sense of 'to cast a blot upon a reputation' (*O.E.D.*).

MICHAEL

Why, that you painters paint lambs in the lining of wenches'
petticoats, and we servingmen put horns to them to make
them become sheep.

CLARKE

Such another word will cost you a cuff or a knock.

MICHAEL

What, with a dagger made of a pencil? Faith, 'tis too weak,   70
and therefore thou too weak to win Susan.

CLARKE

Would Susan's love lay upon this stroke!
                Then he breaks MICHAEL'S *head*
                Here enters MOSBY, GREENE *and* ALICE

ALICE

I'll lay my life this is for Susan's love.
[*To* MICHAEL] Stayed you behind your master to this end?
Have you no other time to brabble in   75
But now, when serious matters are in hand?
                          [*Exit* MICHAEL]
Say, Clarke, hast thou done the thing thou promised?

CLARKE

Ay, here it is; the very touch is death.   [*Exit* CLARKE]

ALICE

Then this, I hope, if all the rest do fail,
Will catch Master Arden   80
And make him wise in death that lived a fool.
Why should he thrust his sickle in our corn, — sexual
Or what hath he to do with thee, my love,
Or govern me that am to rule myself?
Forsooth, for credit sake I must leave thee!   85
Nay, he must leave to live that we may love,

69 *cuff* blow
73 *lay* bet   78 *it* i.e. the poisoned crucifix (see I, 609ff.)
75 *brabble* brawl   86 *leave* cease

66–8 The meaning is obscure. Wine suggests it is a 'proverbial allusion to the
horns of the cuckold', but the idea of sexual rivalry between Clarke and Michael
(which parallels that of Arden and Mosby), is clearer if *horn* is glossed as 'erect
penis' (see E. Partridge, *Shakespeare's Bawdy*, 1961, p. 129). Michael's taunt,
therefore, is that while Clarke is occupied with decorating Susan's petticoat (the
front panel of which would possibly have been visible), Michael is proving his
manhood in a rather more direct manner.

72 s.d. indicates a stage fight

76, 78 s.d.s I have suggested these exits as the closing moments of the scene are
better focused if only Alice, Mosby and Greene remain on stage.

May live, may love; for what is life but love?
And love shall last as long as life remains,
And life shall end before my love depart.
MOSBY
Why, what's love without true constancy?   90
Like to a pillar built of many stones,
Yet neither with good mortar well compact,
Nor cement to fasten it in the joints,
But what it shakes with every blast of wind,
And being touched, straight falls unto the earth   95
And buries all his haughty pride in dust.
No, let our love be rocks of adamant
Which time nor place nor tempest can asunder.
GREENE
Mosby, leave protestations now,
And let us bethink us what we have to do.   100
Black Will and Shakebag I have placed
In the broom close, watching Arden's coming.
Let's to them and see what they have done.   *Exeunt*

Scene XI

Here enters ARDEN *and* FRANKLIN

ARDEN
Oh ferryman, where art thou?
                Here enters the FERRYMAN
FERRYMAN
Here, here! Go before to the boat, and I will follow you.
ARDEN
We have great haste; I pray thee come away.
FERRYMAN
Fie, what a mist is here!
ARDEN
This mist, my friend, is mystical,   5
Like to a good companion's smoky brain
That was half-drowned with new ale overnight.
FERRYMAN
'Twere pity but his skull were opened to make more
chimney room.

93 *cement* Q3 (semell Q1 – 2)

---

8 *but* unless

FRANKLIN
Friend, what's thy opinion of this mist?   10
FERRYMAN
I think 'tis like to a curst wife in a little house, that never
leaves her husband till she have driven him out at doors with
a wet pair of eyes. Then looks he as if his house were afire, or
some of his friends dead.
ARDEN
Speaks thou this of thine own experience?   15
FERRYMAN
Perhaps ay, perhaps no; for my wife is as other women are,
that is to say, governed by the moon.
FRANKLIN
By the moon? How, I pray thee?
FERRYMAN
Nay, thereby lies a bargain, and you shall not have it fresh
and fasting.   20
ARDEN
Yes, I pray thee, good ferryman.
FERRYMAN
Then for this once let it be midsummer moon; but yet my
wife has another moon.
FRANKLIN
Another moon?
FERRYMAN
Ay, and it hath influences and eclipses.   25
ARDEN
Why then, by this reckoning you sometimes play the man in
the moon.

11 *curst* shrewish
12 *at* of
19-20 *fresh and fasting* ?for nothing (so Baskervill, cited by Wine)

---

17 *governed by the moon* cf. proverb, 'As changeful (inconstant) as the moon'
(Tilley, M1111). Jackson (p. 77) notes the possible allusion to the menstrual
cycle (see 11.25 – 6 below).
22 *midsummer moon* 'The lunar month in which Midsummer Day comes;
sometimes alluded to as a time when lunacy is supposed to be prevalent'
(*O.E.D.*). The Ferryman seems to be saying: 'Then just this once I'll be mad
and tell you the jest for nothing.'
23 *another moon* i.e., her sexual organs.
25 *influences and eclipses* obvious sexual connotations.
26 – 7 *man in the moon* again, the sexual allusion is obvious.

FERRYMAN

Ay, but you had not best to meddle with that moon lest I
scratch you by the face with my bramble-bush.

ARDEN

I am almost stifled with this fog; come, let's away.   30

FRANKLIN

And sirrah, as we go, let us have some more of your bold
yeomanry.

FERRYMAN

Nay, by my troth, sir, but flat knavery.   *Exeunt*

Scene XII

Here enters [BLACK] WILL *at one door and*
SHAKEBAG *at another*

SHAKEBAG

Oh Will, where art thou?

BLACK WILL

Here, Shakebag, almost in hell's mouth, where I cannot see
my way for smoke.

SHAKEBAG

I pray thee speak still that we may meet by the sound, for I
shall fall into some ditch or other unless my feet see better   5
than my eyes.

BLACK WILL

Didst thou ever see better weather to run away with another
man's wife or play with a wench at potfinger?

SHAKEBAG

No; this were a fine world for chandlers if this weather
would last, for then a man should never dine nor sup without   10
candle-light. But, sirrah Will, what horses are those that
passed?

31-2 *bold yeomanry* honest, homely speech

---

29 *bramble bush* Cf. *A Midsummer Night's Dream*, V.i, 250‒2, 'All that I have to
say, is, to tell you that the lanthorn is the moon; I, the man i' the moon; this
thorn-bush, my thorn-bush; and this dog, my dog.'

30 The preceding lines, which play obliquely on the idea of a man's wife
cuckolding him, apparently cause Arden to stop the joking and exit abruptly.

8 *potfinger* obvious sexual allusion (*O.E.D.* quotes Withals *Dictionary*, 1666: 'A
potte made in the mouthe, with one finger, as children vse to do'.)

BLACK WILL
Why, didst thou hear any?

SHAKEBAG
Ay, that I did.

BLACK WILL
My life for thine, 'twas Arden and his companion, and then   15
all our labour's lost.

SHAKEBAG
Nay, say not so; for if it be they, they may haply lose their
way as we have done, and then we may chance meet with
them.

BLACK WILL
Come, let us go on like a couple of blind pilgrims.   20

Then SHAKEBAG *falls into a ditch*

SHAKEBAG
Help, Will, help! I am almost drowned.

Here enters the FERRYMAN

FERRYMAN
Who's that that calls for help?

BLACK WILL
'Twas none here; 'twas thou thyself.

FERRYMAN
I came to help him that called for help. Why, how now?
Who is this that's in the ditch? You are well enough served   25
to go without a guide such weather as this!

BLACK WILL
Sirrah, what companies hath passed your ferry this morning?

FERRYMAN
None but a couple of gentlemen that went to dine at my
Lord Cheiny's.

BLACK WILL
Shakebag, did I not tell thee as much?   30

FERRYMAN
Why, sir, will you have any letters carried to them?

BLACK WILL
No, sir; get you gone.

FERRYMAN
Did you ever see such a mist as this?

---

26 *to go* for going
27 *companies* groups of people (Q2 and Q3 read *companions*)

---

20 s.d. *a ditch* possibly Shakebag falls through the trap door of the stage (though see
G. Wickham, *Shakespeare's Dramatic Heritage,* 1969, p. 126). More simply,
Shakebag might just fall to the floor.

BLACK WILL

    No, nor such a fool as will rather be hocked than get his way.

FERRYMAN

    Why, sir, this is no Hock Monday; you are deceived. What's   35
    his name, I pray you, sir?

SHAKEBAG

    His name is Black Will.

FERRYMAN

    I hope to see him one day hanged upon a hill.

                              Exit FERRYMAN

SHAKEBAG

    See how the sun hath cleared the foggy mist,
    Now we have missed the mark of our intent.   40

          Here enters GREENE, MOSBY, *and* ALICE

MOSBY

    Black Will and Shakebag, what make you here?
    What, is the deed done? Is Arden dead?

BLACK WILL

    What could a blinded man perform in arms?
    Saw you not how till now the sky was dark,
    That neither horse nor man could be discerned?   45
    Yet did we hear their horses as they passed.

GREENE

    Have they escaped you then and passed the ferry?

SHAKEBAG

    Ay, for a while; but here we two will stay,
    And at their coming back meet with them once more.
    Zounds, I was ne'er so toiled in all my life   50
    In following so slight a task as this.

MOSBY

    How cam'st thou so bewrayed?

BLACK WILL

    With making false footing in the dark;
    He needs would follow them without a guide.

---

34 *hocked* ed. (hought Qq)
50 *toiled* exhausted, worn out
52 *berayed* covered in mud

---

35 *Hock Monday* a festival held the second Monday (and Tuesday) after Easter,
    during which the women caught (or 'hocked') the men, and made them pay a
    ransom for their freedom. (See Bluestone's discussion of the connection of this
    with the *net* images throughout the play, pp. 178–9.)

ALICE
  Here's to pay for a fire and good cheer.   55
  Get you to Faversham, to the Flower-de-Luce,
  And rest yourselves until some other time.
GREENE
  Let me alone; it most concerns my state.
BLACK WILL
  Ay, Mistress Arden, this will serve the turn
  In case we fall into a second fog.   60
        Exeunt GREENE, [BLACK] WILL *and* SHAKEBAG
MOSBY
  These knaves will never do it; let us give it over.
ALICE
  First tell me how you like my new device:
  Soon, when my husband is returning back,
  You and I both marching arm in arm,
  Like loving friends, we'll meet him on the way,   65
  And boldy beard and brave him to his teeth.
  When words grow hot and blows begin to rise,
  I'll call those cutters forth your tenement,
  Who, in a manner to take up the fray,
  Shall wound my husband Hornsby to the death.   70
MOSBY
  Ah, fine device! Why, this deserves a kiss.   *Exeunt*

Scene XIII

Here enters DICK REEEDE *and a* SAILOR

SAILOR
  Faith, Dick Reede, it is to little end.
  His conscience is too liberal and he too niggardly

62 *device* scheme, plan
66 *beard* affront
68 *tenement* dwelling-place
70 *Hornsby* i.e. the cuckold (see XIII, 82)

---

58 *Let me alone* either; 'Leave me alone to deal with them', or: 'Let me be the one to
  take care of things'.

2 *liberal* 'Free from restraint. . . .In 16-17th c. often in a bad sense: unrestrained
  by prudence or decorum, licentious' (*O.E.D.*).

To part from anything may do thee good.

REEDE

He is coming from Shorlow as I understand.
Here I'll intercept him, for at his house   5
He never will vouchsafe to speak with me.
If prayers and fair entreaties will not serve
Or make no batt'ry in his flinty breast,

Here enters FRANKLIN, ARDEN, *and* MICHAEL

I'll curse the carl and see what that will do.
See where he comes to further my intent. —   10
Master Arden, I am now bound to the sea.
My coming to you was about the plot of ground
Which wrongfully you detain from me.
Although the rent of it be very small,
Yet will it help my wife and children,   15
Which here I leave in Faversham, God knows,
Needy and bare. For Christ's sake, let them have it!

ARDEN

Franklin, hearest thou this fellow speak?
That which he craves I dearly bought of him
Although the rent of it was ever mine.   20
Sirrah, you that ask these questions,
If with thy clamorous impeaching tongue
Thou rail on me as I have heard thou dost,
I'll lay thee up so close a twelve month's day
As thou shalt neither see the sun nor moon.   25
Look to it; for, as surely as I live,
I'll banish pity if thou use me thus.

REEDE

What, wilt thou do me wrong and threat me too?
Nay then, I'll tempt thee, Arden; do thy worst.
God, I beseech thee, show some miracle   30
On thee or thine in plaguing thee for this.
That plot of ground which thou detains from me —
I speak it in an agony of spirit —
Be ruinous and fatal unto thee!
Either there be butchered by thy dearest friends,   35
Or else be brought for men to wonder at,
Or thou or thine miscarry in that place,

9 *carl* miserly fellow
24 *lay . . . close* imprison you
29 *tempt* provoke
37 *miscarry* come to harm, die

Or there run mad and end thy cursed days.

FRANKLIN

Fie, bitter knave, bridle thine envious tongue;
For curses are like arrows shot upright,   40
Which, falling down, light on the shooter's head.

REEDE

Light where they will! Were I upon the sea,
As oft I have in many a bitter storm,
And saw a dreadful southern flaw at hand,
The pilot quaking at the doubtful storm,   45
And all the sailors praying on their knees,
Even in that fearful time would I fall down
And ask of God, whate'er betide of me,
Vengeance on Arden, or some misevent,
To show the world what wrong the carl hath done.   50
This charge I'll leave with my distressful wife;
My children shall be taught such prayers as these.
And thus I go, but leave my curse with thee,

                                        Exeunt REEDE *and* SAILOR

ARDEN

It is the railingest knave in Christendom,
And oftentimes the villain will be mad.   55
It greatly matters not what he says,
But I assure you I ne'er did him wrong.

FRANKLIN

I think so, Master Arden.

ARDEN

Now that our horses are gone home before,
My wife may haply meet me on the way;   60
For God knows she is grown passing kind of late
And greatly changed from the old humour
Of her wonted frowardness,
And seeks by fair means to redeem old faults.

FRANKLIN

Happy the change that alters for the best.   65
But see in any case you make no speech
Of the cheer we had at my Lord Cheiny's —
Although most bounteous and liberal —

For that will make her think herself more wronged
In that we did not carry her along;   70
For sure she grieved that she was left behind.

ARDEN

Come, Franklin, let us strain to mend our pace
And take her unawares, playing the cook,
>   *Here enters* ALICE *and* MOSBY [*arm in arm*]
For I believe she'll strive to mend our cheer.

FRANKLIN

Why, there's no better creatures in the world   75
Than women are when they are in good humours.

ARDEN

Who is that? Mosby? What, so familiar?
Injurious strumpet and thou ribald knave,
Untwine those arms.

ALICE

Ay, with a sugared kiss let them untwine.   80

ARDEN

Ah, Mosby! Perjured beast! Bear this and all!

MOSBY

And yet no horned beast; the horns are thine.

FRANKLIN

Oh monstrous! Nay then, 'tis time to draw!

ALICE

Help! Help! They murder my husband!
>   *Here enters* [BLACK] WILL *and* SHAKEBAG

SHAKEBAG

Zounds, who injures Master Mosby?   85
>   [*They fight.* SHAKEBAG *and* MOSBY *are wounded*]
Help, Will, I am hurt.

MOSBY

I may thank you, Mistress Arden, for this wound.
>   *Exeunt* MOSBY, [BLACK] WILL, *and* SHAKEBAG

ALICE

Ah, Arden, what folly blinded thee?
Ah, jealous harebrain man what hast thou done?
When we, to welcome thee, intended sport,   90
Came lovingly to meet thee on thy way,
Thou drew'st thy sword, enraged with jealousy,
And hurt thy friend whose thoughts were free from harm;
All for a worthless kiss and joining arms,

72 *mend* increase
78 *ribald* scurrilous
82 *horned beast* i.e., cuckold

Both done but merrily to try thy patience.   95
And me unhappy that devised the jest,
Which, though begun in sport, yet ends in blood!

FRANKLIN
Marry, God defend me from such a jest!

ALICE
Couldst thou not see us friendly smile on thee
When we joined arms and when I kissed his cheek?   100
Hast thou not lately found me over-kind?
Didst thou not hear me cry they murder thee?
Called I not help to set my husband free?
No, ears and all were 'witched. Ah me accursed,
To link in liking with a frantic man!   105
Henceforth I'll be thy slave, no more thy wife;
For with that name I never shall content thee.
If I be merry, thou straightways thinks me light;
If sad, thou sayest the sullens trouble me;
If well attired, thou thinks I will be gadding;   110
If homely, I seem sluttish in thine eye.
Thus am I still, and shall be while I die,
Poor wench abused by thy misgovernment.

ARDEN
But is it for truth that neither thou nor he
Intendedst malice in your misdemeanour?   115

ALICE
The heavens can witness of our harmless thoughts.

ARDEN
Then pardon me, sweet Alice, and forgive this fault;
Forget but this, and never see the like.
Impose me penance, and I will perform it;
For in thy discontent I find a death,   120
A death tormenting more than death itself.

ALICE
Nay, hadst thou loved me as thou dost pretend,
Thou wouldst have marked the speeches of thy friend,
Who going wounded from the place, he said
His skin was pierced only through my device.   125
And if sad sorrow taint thee for this fault
Thou wouldst have followed him and seen him dressed,
And cried him mercy whom thou hast misdone;

109 *sullens* sulks   *while* until
112 *still* always   128 *misdone* wronged, injured

127 *him* i.e., his wounds

Ne'er shall my heart be eased till this be done.

ARDEN

    Content thee, sweet Alice, thou shalt have thy will,   130
    Whate'er it be. For that I injured thee
    And wronged my friend, shame scourgeth my offence.
    Come thou thyself and go along with me,
    And be a mediator 'twixt us two.

FRANKLIN

    Why, Master Arden, know you what you do?   135
    Will you follow him that hath dishonoured you?

ALICE

    Why, canst thou prove I have been disloyal?

FRANKLIN

    Why, Mosby taunts your husband with the horn.

ALICE

    Ay, after he had reviled him
    By the injurious name of perjured beast.   140
    He knew no wrong could spite a jealous man
    More than the hateful naming of the horn.

FRANKLIN

    Suppose 'tis true, yet is it dangerous
    To follow him whom he hath lately hurt.

ALICE

    A fault confessed is more than half amends,   145
    But men of such ill spirit as yourself
    Work crosses and debates 'twixt man and wife.

ARDEN

    I pray thee, gentle Franklin, hold thy peace;
    I know my wife counsels me for the best.
    I'll seek out Mosby where his wound is dressed   150
    And salve his hapless quarrel if I may.

                        Exeunt ARDEN *and* ALICE

FRANKLIN

    He whom the devil drives must go perforce.
    Poor gentleman, how soon he is bewitched.
    And yet, because his wife is the instrument,
    His friends must not be lavish in their speech.   155

                            Exit FRANKLIN

131 *For that* because
138 *taunts your* Q3 (traunt you Q1; taunt you Q2)
151 *hapless* unfortunate

Scene XIV

Here enters [BLACK] WILL, SHAKEBAG, *and* GREENE

BLACK WILL
Sirrah Greene, when was I so long in killing a man?
GREENE
I think we shall never do it; let us give it over.
SHAKEBAG
Nay! Zounds, we'll kill him though we be hanged at his door
for our labour.
BLACK WILL
Thou knowest, Greene, that I have lived in London this   5
twelve years, where I have made some go upon wooden legs
for taking the wall on me; divers with silver noses for saying,
'There goes Black Will.' I have cracked as many blades as
thou hast done nuts.
GREENE
Oh, monstrous lie!   10
BLACK WILL
Faith, in a manner I have. The bawdy-houses have paid me
tribute; there durst not a whore set up unless she have agreed
with me first for opening her shop windows. For a cross
word of a tapster I have pierced one barrel after another with
my dagger and held him by the ears till all his beer hath run   15
out. In Thames Street a brewer's cart was like to have run
over me; I made no more ado but went to the clerk and cut
all the notches off his tallies and beat them about his head. I
and my company have taken the constable from his watch
and carried him about the fields on a coltstaff. I have broken   20
a sergeant's head with his own mace, and bailed whom I list
with my sword and buckler. All the tenpenny alehouses
would stand every morning with a quart pot in their hand,

7 *silver noses* i.e. false noses   21 *list* wished, chose
18 *tallies* ed. (tales Qq)   23 *their* Q2–3 (his Q1)
21 *mace* staff of office

7 *taking the wall* i.e., taking the side of the street nearest the wall (thereby forcing
   Black Will into the middle of the street where it was filthiest).
18 *tallies* sticks of wood marked on one side with notches representing the amount
   of a debt or payment.
20 *coltstaff* (or cowlstaff): a pole used for carrying a cowl (tub); *O.E.D.* notes, 'It
   was a familiar household requisite, and a ready weapon.'
21 *sergeant* officer responsible for arresting offenders or summoning them to court.
22 *tenpenny alehouses* i.e., the keepers of alehouses where ale was sold for tenpence
   a quart.

saying, 'Will it please your worship drink?' He that had not
done so had been sure to have had his sign pulled down and   25
his lattice borne away the next night. To conclude, what
have I not done? Yet cannot do this; doubtless he is
preserved by miracle.

Here enters ALICE *and* MICHAEL

GREENE
Hence, Will; here comes Mistress Arden.
ALICE
Ah, gentle Michael, art thou sure they're friends?   30
MICHAEL
Why, I saw them when they both shook hands;
When Mosby bled he even wept for sorrow,
And railed on Franklin that was cause of all.
No sooner came the surgeon in at doors,
But my master took his purse and gave him money,   35
And, to conclude, sent me to bring you word
That Mosby, Franklin, Bradshaw, Adam Fowle,
With divers of his neighbours and his friends,
Will come and sup with you at our house this night.
ALICE
Ah, gentle Michael, run thou back again,   40
And when my husband walks into the fair,
Bid Mosby steal from him and come to me;
And this night shall thou and Susan be made sure.
MICHAEL
I'll go tell him.
ALICE
And as thou goest, tell John cook of our guests,   45
And bid him lay it on; spare for no cost.   *Exit* MICHAEL
BLACK WILL
Nay, and there be such cheer, we will bid ourselves.
Mistress Arden, Dick Greene and I do mean to sup with
you.
ALICE
And welcome shall you be. Ah, gentlemen,   50
How missed you of your purpose yesternight?

46 *lay it on* provide generous hospitality   47 *and* if
                                                 bid invite

26 *lattice* a window of lattice work painted either red or green was the sign of an
   alehouse.
41 *the fair* i.e., of St Valentine. See Intro., p. xii.
45 *John cook* i.e., John, the cook.

GREENE

'Twas long of Shakebag, that unlucky villain.

SHAKEBAG

Thou dost me wrong; I did as much as any.

BLACK WILL

Nay then, Mistress Alice, I'll tell you how it was. When he
should have locked with both his hilts, he in a bravery   55
flourished over his head. With that comes Franklin at him
lustily and hurts the slave; with that he slinks away. Now his
way had been to have come in hand and feet, one and two
round at his costard. He like a fool bears his sword-point half
a yard out of danger. I lie here for my life. [*He takes up a*   60
position of defence.] If the devil come and he have no more
strength than fence, he shall never beat me from this ward;
I'll stand to it. A buckler in a skilful hand is as good as a
castle; nay, 'tis better than a sconce, for I have tried it.
Mosby, perceiving this, began to faint. With that comes   65
Arden with his arming-sword and thrust him through the
shoulder in a trice.

52 *long of* on account of
55 *locked* attacked, crossed swords
55 *in a bravery* with a show of bravado
58 *in* ed., (not in Qq)
   round directly
59 *costard* head (really an apple, but often applied humorously or derisively to the
   head)
62 *fence* fencing skill
62 *ward* defensive posture
63 *buckler* small round shield
64 *sconce* small fort
65 *faint* lose heart or courage

---

55 *hilts* The hilt of a sword being divided in three parts—pommel, handle, and
   shell—could be spoken of as plural (eg., *1 Henry IV*, II.iv, 202). Here, however,
   it probably refers to Shakebag's sword and dagger.
58 *come in* 'to make a pass or home thrust, to get within the opponent's guard' (see *1
   Henry IV*, II.iv, 209 – 10).
63 *I'll stand to it* i.e., 'I'll fight fiercely to maintain it'. Punctuated differently, so
   that it becomes part of the next sentence, the phrase would mean 'I'll maintain
   that'. See Wine, who punctuates in this alternative way.
65 *this* i.e., Shakebag's injury and defeat.
66 *arming-sword* sometimes glossed as 'broad sword', but more likely 'the sword
   with which he was armed'. See *O.E.D.* 1.b., 'Forming part of arms or armour'.

ALICE

Ay, but I wonder why you both stood still.

BLACK WILL

Faith, I was so amazed I could not strike.

ALICE

Ah, sirs, had he yesternight been slain,   70
For every drop of his detested blood
I would have crammed in angels in thy fist,
And kissed thee, too, and hugged thee in my arms.

BLACK WILL

Patient yourself; we cannot help it now.
Greene and we two will dog him through the fair,   75
And stab him in the crowd, and steal away.

Here enters MOSBY [, *his arm bandaged*]

ALICE

It is unpossible. But here comes he
That will, I hope, invent some surer means.
Sweet Mosby, hide thy arm; it kills my heart.

MOSBY

Ay, Mistress Arden, this is your favour.   80

ALICE

Ah, say not so; for when I saw thee hurt
I could have took the weapon thou let'st fall
And run at Arden, for I have sworn
That these mine eyes, offended with his sight,
Shall never close till Arden's be shut up.   85
This night I rose and walked about the chamber,
And twice or thrice I thought to have murdered him.

MOSBY

What, in the night? Then had we been undone!

ALICE

Why, how long shall he live?

MOSBY

Faith, Alice, no longer than this night.   90
Black Will and Shakebag, will you two
Perform the complot that I have laid?

BLACK WILL

Ay, or else think me as a villain.

72 *have crammed in angels* Q3 (cramme in Angels Q1; have camd in angels Q2)
74 *Patient yourself* calm yourself, be patient
86 *This night* i.e. last night

80 *favour* a gift 'given to a lover. . .to be worn conspicuously as a token of
affection' (*O.E.D.*, sb.,7).

GREENE
> And rather than you shall want, I'll help myself.

MOSBY
> You, Master Greene, shall single Franklin forth   95
> And hold him with a long tale of strange news,
> That he may not come home till suppertime.
> I'll fetch Master Arden home, and we, like friends,
> Will play a game or two at tables here.

ALICE
> But what of all this? How shall he be slain?   100

MOSBY
> Why, Black Will and Shakebag, locked within the
>   countinghouse,
> Shall, at a certain watchword given, rush forth.

BLACK WILL
> What shall the watchword be?

MOSBY
> 'Now I take you' — that shall be the word.
> But come not forth before in any case.   105

BLACK WILL
> I warrant you; but who shall lock me in?

ALICE
> That will I do; thou'st keep the key thyself.

MOSBY
> Come, Master Greene, go you along with me.
> See all things ready, Alice, against we come.

ALICE
> Take no care for that; send you him home.   110

Exeunt MOSBY *and* GREENE

> And if he e'er go forth again blame me.
> Come, Black Will, that in mine eyes art fair;
> Next unto Mosby do I honour thee.
> Instead of fair words and large promises
> My hands shall play you golden harmony.   115
> How like you this? Say, will you do it, sirs?

94 *want* fail (*O.E.D.,* v.I.†d)
99 *tables* backgammon
101 *countinghouse* private room used as an office
109 *against* by the time that, before
110 *Take . . .that* don't worry about that, leave that to me
117 *bravely* excellently, splendidly

115 *my. . .harmony* i.e., 'I'll give you gold crowns.' (See III, 89–92.)

BLACK WILL

Ay, and that bravely, too. Mark my device:
Place Mosby, being a stranger, in a chair,
And let your husband sit upon a stool,
That I may come behind him cunningly   120
And with a towel pull him to the ground,
Then stab him till his flesh be as a sieve.
That done, bear him behind the Abbey,
That those that find him murdered may suppose
Some slave or other killed him for his gold.   125

ALICE

A fine device! You shall have twenty pound,
And when he is dead you shall have forty more.
And lest you might be suspected staying here,
Michael shall saddle you two lusty geldings.
Ride whither you will, to Scotland or to Wales,   130
I'll see you shall not lack where'er you be.

BLACK WILL

Such words would make one kill a thousand men!
Give me the key; which is the countinghouse?

ALICE

Here would I stay and still encourage you,
But that I know how resolute you are.   135

SHAKEBAG

Tush! You are too faint-hearted; we must do it.

ALICE

But Mosby will be there, whose very looks
Will add unwonted courage to my thought,
And make me the first that shall adventure on him.

BLACK WILL

Tush, get you gone; 'tis we must do the deed.   140

---

122 *sieve* Q2 (siue) Q3 (sive) (sine Q1)
139 *adventure on* attack

118– 19 Wine quotes M. Jourdain, *English Decoration and Furniture of the Early
*   Renaissance* (1500– 1650), 1924, p. 241: 'This scarcity of chairs is due to their
rarity during the early Renaissance. Stools and forms outnumbered the chairs in
hall and parlour until the Restoration....In domestic use the chair was the
rightful seat of the master of the house, only given up by courtesy.' (See below,
1.287.)
122 Sturgess notes that 'seine' (sine Q1), a fishing net 'is marginally possible.'See
also note to XII, 37.

When this door opens next, look for his death.

[Exeunt BLACK WILL *and* SHAKEBAG]

ALICE

Ah, would he now were here, that it might open.
I shall no more be closed in Arden's arms,
That like the snakes of black Tisiphone
Sting me with their embracings. Mosby's arms   145
Shall compass me, and, were I made a star,
I would have none other spheres but those.
There is no nectar but in Mosby's lips!
Had chaste Diana kissed him, she like me
Would grow love-sick, and from her wat'ry bower   150
Fling down Endymion and snatch him up.
Then blame not me that slay a silly man
Not half so lovely as Endymion.

Here enters MICHAEL

MICHAEL

Mistress, my master is coming hard by.

ALICE

Who comes with him?   155

MICHAEL

Nobody but Mosby.

ALICE

That's well, Michael. Fetch in the tables; and, when thou
hast done, stand before the countinghouse door.

MICHAEL

Why so?

ALICE

Black Will is locked within to do the deed.   160

MICHAEL

What, shall he die tonight?

---

145 *embracings* Q2–3 (enbraceings Q1)
151 *snatch* Q2–3 (snath Q1)

---

143 *Tisiphone* One of the Furies who pursued those who committed crimes against
their kin. Their hair and arms were encircled with snakes, and each carried a
torch and a whip to sting the consciences of the guilty.

151 *Endymion* A beautiful mortal with whom Diana, the goddess of the moon, fell
in love.

142–153 This speech, with its ironic and hyperbolic comparisons, reveals
strikingly the widening gap between Alice's own perceptions of her actions and
their real nature. (See also Ousby, p. 52.)

ALICE
  Ay, Michael.
MICHAEL
  But shall not Susan know it?
ALICE
  Yes, for she'll be as secret as ourselves.
MICHAEL
  That's brave! I'll go fetch the tables.   165
ALICE
  But Michael, hark to me a word or two:
  When my husband is come in, lock the street door;
  He shall be murdered ere the guests come in.
          Exit MICHAEL [*and re-enter with the tables*]
          Here enters ARDEN *and* MOSBY
  Husband, what mean you to bring Mosby home?
  Although I wished you to be reconciled,   170
  'Twas more for fear of you than love of him.
  Black Will and Greene are his companions,
  And they are cutters and may cut you short;
  Therefore, I thought it good to make you friends.
  But wherefore do you bring him hither now?   175
  You have given me my supper with his sight.
MOSBY
  Master Arden, methinks your wife would have me gone.
ARDEN
  No, good Master Mosby, women will be prating.
  Alice, bid him welcome; he and I are friends.
ALICE
  You may enforce me to it if you will,   180
  But I had rather die than bid him welcome.
  His company hath purchased me ill friends,
  And therefore will I ne'er frequent it more.
MOSBY
  [*Aside*] Oh, how cunningly she can dissemble!

165 *brave* splendid
168 *ere* Q3 (or Q1–2) before
171 *of you* i.e. for you

---

172 *Greene* One would, as Sturgess observes, 'expect "Shakebag", not "Greene",
    at this point. Greene is not a "cutter", and it was Shakebag, not Greene,
    involved with Mosby and Black Will in the scuffle of scene XIII.' Sturgess
    points out that 'Greene' suits   the rhythm of the line better, but, I suggest, it
    may well be a dangerous slip on Alice's part that momentarily chills the hearts
    of her accomplices.

ARDEN

  Now he is here, you will not serve me so.   185

ALICE

  I pray you be not angry or displeased;

  I'll bid him welcome, seeing you'll have it so:

  You are welcome, Master Mosby. Will you sit down?

MOSBY

  I know I am welcome to your loving husband,

  But for yourself you speak not from your heart.   190

ALICE

  And if I do not, sir, think I have cause.

MOSBY

  Pardon me, Master Arden, I'll away.

ARDEN

  No, good Master Mosby.

ALICE

  We shall have guests enough though you go hence.

MOSBY

  I pray you, Master Arden, let me go.   195

ARDEN

  I pray thee, Mosby, let her prate her fill.

ALICE

  The doors are open, sir; you may be gone.

MICHAEL

  [*Aside*] Nay, that's a lie, for I have locked the doors.

ARDEN

  Sirrah, fetch me a cup of wine; I'll make them friends.

                             [*Exit* MICHAEL]

  And, gentle Mistress Alice, seeing you are so stout,   200

  You shall begin. Frown not; I'll have it so.

ALICE

  I pray you meddle with that you have to do.

ARDEN

  Why, Alice, how can I do too much for him

  Whose life I have endangered without cause?

                 [*Enter* MICHAEL *with wine*]

ALICE

  'Tis true; and seeing 'twas partly through my means,   205

  I am content to drink to him for this once.

192 *Master* ed. (M. Q1 – 2; mistris Q3)
200 *stout* stubborn
201 *begin* i.e. make the first toast

---

198 Michael, who exited at 1.168, must re-enter at some point before his line.

Here, Master Mosby! And, I pray you, henceforth
Be you as strange to me as I to you.
Your company hath purchased me ill friends,
And I for you, God knows, have undeserved   210
Been ill spoken of in every place;
Therefore, henceforth frequent my house no more.

MOSBY

I'll see your husband in despite of you.
Yet, Arden, I protest to thee by heaven,
Thou ne'er shalt see me more after this night.   215
I'll go to Rome rather than be forsworn.

ARDEN

Tush, I'll have no such vows made in my house.

ALICE

Yes, I pray you, husband, let him swear;
And on that condition, Mosby, pledge me here.

MOSBY

Ay, as willingly as I mean to live.   220

ARDEN

Come, Alice, is our supper ready yet?

ALICE

It will by then you have played a game at tables.

ARDEN

Come, Master Mosby, what shall we play for?

MOSBY

Three games for a French crown, sir, and please you.

ARDEN

Content.   225

Then they play at the tables
[*Enter* BLACK WILL *and* SHAKEBAG]

BLACK WILL

[*Aside*] Can he not take him yet? What a spite is that!

ALICE

[*Aside*] Not yet, Will. Take heed he see thee not.

BLACK WILL

[*Aside*] I fear he will spy me as I am coming.

MICHAEL

[*Aside*] To prevent that, creep betwixt my legs.

MOSBY

One ace, or else I lose the game.   [*He throws the dice*]   230

219 *pledge* drink to
230 *ace* side of the dice marked with a single dot

ARDEN

Marry, sir, there's two for failing.

MOSBY

Ah, Master Arden, 'Now I can take you.'

Then [BLACK] WILL *pulls him down with a towel*

ARDEN

Mosby! Michael! Alice! What will you do?

BLACK WILL

Nothing but take you up, sir, nothing else.

MOSBY

There's for the pressing iron you told me of.   235

[*He hits him with the iron*]

SHAKEBAG

And there's for the ten pound in my sleeve.   [*Stabs him*]

ALICE

What, groans thou? Nay then, give me the weapon.

Take this for hind'ring Mosby's love and mine.

[*Stabs him*]

MICHAEL

Oh, Mistress!   [ARDEN *dies*]

BLACK WILL

Ah, that villain will betray us all.   240

MOSBY

Tush, fear him not; he will be secret.

MICHAEL

Why, dost thou think I will betray myself?

SHAKEBAG

In Southwark dwells a bonny northern lass,

The widow Chambley; I'll to her house now,

And if she will not give me harborough,   245

I'll make booty of the quean, even to her smock.

245 *harborough* harbour, shelter
246 *quean* strumpet, harlot

---

231 *for failing* i.e., 'in case one is not enough' (see *for*, I, 225).

234 *take you up* deal with you (playing on the 'watchword').

235 In Holinshed, Mosby 'hauing at his girdle a pressing iron of fourteen pounds weight, stroke him on the hed with the same, so that he fell downe, and gaue a great grone, insomuch that they thought he had beene killed.' The playwright picks up the 'grone' at 1.237, so perhaps he also intended that Mosby should kill Arden with an iron. There is no stage direction in Qq. (See Intro., p. xxvi.)

237 *the weapon* presumably Shakebag's sword or dagger.

243 *Southwark* 'A borough, formerly independent of the London city government,' where most of the playhouses were erected (the Globe, the Rose, the Swan, etc.) as well as the bear-baiting ring at Paris Garden (Sugden).

BLACK WILL
  Shift for yourselves; we two will leave you now.
ALICE
  First lay the body in the countinghouse.
          Then they lay the body in the countinghouse
BLACK WILL
  We have our gold. Mistress Alice, adieu;
  Mosby, farewell, and Michael, farewell too.   250
                  Exeunt [BLACK WILL *and* SHAKEBAG]
                  Enter SUSAN
SUSAN
  Mistress, the guests are at the doors.
  Hearken, they knock. What, shall I let them in?
ALICE
  Mosby, go thou and bear them company.   *Exit* MOSBY
  And, Susan, fetch water and wash away this blood.
          [*Exit* SUSAN, *returns with water, and washes the floor*]
SUSAN
  The blood cleaveth to the ground and will not out.   255
ALICE
  But with my nails I'll scrape away the blood. —
  The more I strive the more the blood appears!
SUSAN
  What's the reason, Mistress, can you tell?
ALICE
  Because I blush not at my husband's death.
                  Here enters MOSBY
MOSBY
  How now, what's the matter? Is all well?   260
ALICE
  Ay, well, if Arden were alive again!
  In vain we strive, for here his blood remains.
MOSBY
  Why, strew rushes on it, can you not?
  This wench doth nothing; fall unto the work.
ALICE
  'Twas thou that made me murder him.   265
MOSBY   What of that?

254–7 Cf. *Macbeth*, II.ii, 59–60: 'Will all great Neptune's ocean wash this
    blood/Clean from my hand?'
263 *rushes* 'Down to the seventeenth century green rushes were commonly
    employed for strewing on the floors' (*O.E.D.*).

ALICE

Nay, nothing, Mosby, so it be not known.

MOSBY

Keep thou it close, and 'tis unpossible.

ALICE

Ah, but I cannot. Was he not slain by me?

My husband's death torments me at the heart.

MOSBY

It shall not long torment thee, gentle Alice.   270

I am thy husband; think no more on him.

Here enters ADAM FOWLE *and* BRADSHAW

BRADSHAW

How now, Mistress Arden, what ail you weep?

MOSBY

Because her husband is abroad so late.

A couple of ruffians threat'ned him yesternight,

And she, poor soul, is afraid he should be hurt.   275

ADAM

Is't nothing else? Tush, he'll be here anon.

Here enters GREENE

GREENE

Now, Mistress Arden, lack you any guests?

ALICE

Ah, Master Greene, did you see my husband lately?

GREENE

I saw him walking behind the Abbey even now.

Here enters FRANKLIN

ALICE

I do not like this being out so late.   280

Master Franklin, where did you leave my husband?

FRANKLIN

Believe me, I saw him not since morning.

Fear you not, he'll come anon. Meantime,

You may do well to bid his guests sit down.

ALICE

Ay, so they shall. Master Bradshaw, sit you there;   285

I pray you be content, I'll have my will.

Master Mosby, sit you in my husband's seat.

MICHAEL

[*Aside*] Susan, shall thou and I wait on them?

Or, and thou say'st the word, let us sit down too.

267 *close* secret

SUSAN

    [Aside] Peace, we have other matters now in hand.   290

    I fear me, Michael, all will be bewrayed.

MICHAEL

    [Aside] Tush, so it be known that I shall marry thee in the

    morning I care not though I be hanged ere night. But to

    prevent the worst I'll buy some ratsbane.

SUSAN

    [Aside] Why, Michael, wilt thou poison thyself?   295

MICHAEL

    [Aside] No, but my mistress, for I fear she'll tell.

SUSAN

    [Aside] Tush, Michael, fear not her; she's wise enough.

MOSBY

    Sirrah Michael, give's a cup of beer.

    Mistress Arden, here's to your husband.

ALICE

    My husband!   300

FRANKLIN

    What ails you, woman, to cry so suddenly?

ALICE

    Ah, neighbours, a sudden qualm came over my heart;

    My husband's being forth torments my mind.

    I know something's amiss; he is not well,

    Or else I should have heard of him ere now.   305

MOSBY

    [Aside] She will undo us through her foolishness.

GREENE

    Fear not, Mistress Arden, he's well enough.

ALICE

    Tell not me; I know he is not well.

    He was not wont for to stay thus late.

    Good Master Franklin, go and seek him forth,   310

    And if you find him send him home to me,

    And tell him what a fear he hath put me in.

FRANKLIN

    [Aside] I like not this; I pray God all be well. —

    I'll seek him out and find him if I can.

             Exeunt FRANKLIN, MOSBY, *and* GREENE

ALICE

    [Aside] Michael, how shall I do to rid the rest away?   315

291 *bewrayed* betrayed, revealed

294 *ratsbane* rat poison, arsenic

314 *s.d.* after l.313 in Qq

MICHAEL

    [*Aside*] Leave that to my charge; let me alone. —
    'Tis very late, Master Bradshaw,
    And there are many false knaves abroad,
    And you have many narrow lanes to pass.

BRADSHAW

    Faith, friend Michael, and thou sayest true.   320
    Therefore I pray thee light's forth and lend's a link.
            Exeunt BRADSHAW, ADAM [FOWLE], *and* MICHAEL

ALICE

    [*Aside*] Michael, bring them to the doors, but do not stay;
    You know I do not love to be alone. —
    Go, Susan, and bid thy brother come.
    But wherefore should he come? Here is nought but
        fear.   325
    Stay, Susan, stay, and help to counsel me.

SUSAN

    Alas, I counsel! Fear frights away my wits.
        Then they open the countinghouse door and look
                upon ARDEN

ALICE

    See, Susan, where thy quondam master lies;
    Sweet Arden, smeared in blood and filthy gore.

SUSAN

    My brother, you, and I shall rue this deed.   330

ALICE

    Come, Susan, help to lift his body forth.
    And let our salt tears be his obsequies.
        [*They lift his body out of the countinghouse*]
         Here enters MOSBY *and* GREENE

MOSBY

    How now, Alice, whither will you bear him?

ALICE

    Sweet Mosby, art thou come? Then weep that will;
    I have my wish in that I joy thy sight.   335

GREENE

    Well, it 'hoves us to be circumspect.

MOSBY

    Ay, for Franklin thinks that we have murdered him.

ALICE

    Ay, but he cannot prove it for his life.

321 *link* torch
328 *quondam* former
336 *'hoves* behoves

We'll spend this night in dalliance and in sport.

Here enters MICHAEL

MICHAEL

Oh mistress, the mayor and all the watch   340
Are coming towards our house with glaives and bills.

ALICE

Make the door fast; let them not come in.

MOSBY

Tell me, sweet Alice, how shall I escape?

ALICE

Out at the back door, over the pile of wood,
And for one night lie at the Flower-de-Luce.   345

MOSBY

That is the next way to betray myself.

GREENE

Alas, Mistress Arden, the watch will take me here,
And cause suspicion where else would be none.

ALICE

Why, take that way that Master Mosby doth;
But first convey the body to the fields.   350

MOSBY

Until tomorrow, sweet Alice; now farewell,
And see you confess nothing in any case.

GREENE

Be resolute, Mistress Alice; betray us not,
But cleave to us as we will stick to you.

Then they [MOSBY, GREENE, MICHAEL, *and* SUSAN] *bear
the body into the fields*

ALICE

Now let the judge and juries do their worst;   355
My house is clear and now I fear them not.

[*Enter* MICHAEL *and* SUSAN]

SUSAN

As we went it snowed all the way,
Which makes me fear our footsteps will be spied.

341 *glaives* swords
    bills halberds
346 *next* quickest, surest

---

354 s.d. Qq place the stage direction after 1.350, which means that Mosby and
Greene return merely to speak a total of 4 lines before they exit again. In
performance it is more practical if the exit is delayed until 1.354. Alice can then
busy herself with straightening the room ('My house is clear'), until Michael
and Susan return on 1.357. Susan's information is so important that it provides
a good entry line.

ALICE

Peace, fool! The snow will cover them again.

SUSAN

But it had done before we came back again.   360

ALICE

Hark, hark, they knock! Go, Michael, let them in.

[MICHAEL *opens the door*]

Here enters the MAYOR *and the* WATCH

How now, Master Mayor, have you brought my husband
home?

MAYOR

I saw him come into your house an hour ago.

ALICE

You are deceived; it was a Londoner.

MAYOR

Mistress Arden, know you not one that is called Black Will? 365

ALICE

I know none such. What mean these questions?

MAYOR

I have the Council's warrant to apprehend him.

ALICE

[*Aside*] I am glad it is no worse. —

Why, Master Mayor, think you I harbour any such?

MAYOR

We are informed that here he is,   370

And therefore pardon us, for we must search.

ALICE

Ay, search, and spare you not, through every room.

Were my husband at home you would not offer this.

Here enters FRANKLIN

Master Franklin. what mean you come so sad?

FRANKLIN

Arden, thy husband and my friend, is slain.   375

ALICE

Ah, by whom, Master Franklin? Can you tell?

FRANKLIN

I know not; but behind the Abbey

There he lies murdered in most piteous case.

360 *done* i.e. stopped snowing
378 *piteous case* pitiful condition

364 *a Londoner* According to Holinshed, after the murder Alice 'sent for two
    Londoners to supper, the one named Prune, and the other Cole, that were
    grosers'.

MAYOR
But, Master Franklin, are you sure 'tis he?
FRANKLIN
I am too sure; would God I were deceived.   380
ALICE
Find out the murderers; let them be known.
FRANKLIN
Ay, so they shall. Come you along with us.
ALICE
Wherefore?
FRANKLIN
Know you this hand-towel and this knife?
SUSAN
[*Aside*] Ah, Michael, through this thy negligence   385
Thou hast betrayed and undone us all.
MICHAEL
[*Aside*] I was so afraid I knew not what I did.
I thought I had thrown them both into the well.
ALICE
It is the pig's blood we had to supper.
But wherefore stay you? Find out the murderers.   390
MAYOR
I fear me you'll prove one of them yourself.
ALICE
I one of them? What mean such questions?
FRANKLIN
I fear me he was murdered in this house
And carried to the fields, for from that place
Backwards and forwards may you see   395
The print of many feet within the snow.
And look about this chamber where we are,
And you shall find part of his guiltless blood;
For in his slipshoe did I find some rushes,
Which argueth he was murdered in this room.   400
MAYOR
Look in the place where he was wont to sit.
See, see! His blood! It is too manifest.
ALICE
It is a cup of wine that Michael shed.
MICHAEL
Ay, truly.

389 *to* for
399 *slipshoe* slipper

FRANKLIN
    It is his blood which, strumpet, thou hast shed.   405
    But if I live, thou and thy complices
    Which have conspired and wrought his death shall rue it.

ALICE
    Ah, Master Franklin, God and heaven can tell
    I loved him more than all the world beside.
    But bring me to him; let me see his body.   410

FRANKLIN
    Bring that villain and Mosby's sister too;
    And one of you go to the Flower-de-Luce
    And seek for Mosby, and apprehend him too.   *Exeunt*

Scene XV

Here enters SHAKEBAG *solus*

SHAKEBAG
    The widow Chambley in her husband's days I kept;
    And now he's dead she is grown so stout
    She will not know her old companions.
    I came thither, thinking to have had
    Harbour as I was wont,   5
    And she was ready to thrust me out at doors.
    But whether she would or no I got me up,
    And as she followed me I spurned her down the stairs
    And broke her neck, and cut her tapster's throat;
    And now I am going to fling them in the Thames.   10
    I have the gold; what care I though it be known?
    I'll cross the water and take sanctuary.
                   Exit SHAKEBAG

s.d. *solus* alone
  1 *kept* i.e. as a mistress
  2 *stout* proud
  8 *spurned* kicked

411 *that villain* i.e., Michael.

12 *take sanctuary* i.e. seek refuge in one of the areas of a church or royal palace
    where criminals were safe from arrest for crimes other than blasphemy or
    treason. Wine points out that, according to XIV, 243–4, if Shakebag has been
    to the widow Chambley's he is already in Southwark, where the Mint was
    designated a sanctuary, and where he is eventually murdered (see Epilogue,
    3–5).

Scene XVI

Here enters the MAYOR, MOSBY, ALICE, FRANKLIN,
MICHAEL, *and* SUSAN [*guarded by the* WATCH]

MAYOR
  See, Mistress Arden, where your husband lies.
  Confess this foul fault and be penitent.
ALICE
  Arden, sweet husband, what shall I say?
  The more I sound his name the more he bleeds.
  This blood condemns me, and in gushing forth   5
  Speaks as it falls and asks me why I did it.
  Forgive me, Arden; I repent me now;
  And would my death save thine thou shouldst not die.
  Rise up, sweet Arden, and enjoy thy love,
  And frown not on me when we meet in heaven;   10
  In heaven I love thee though on earth I did not.
MAYOR
  Say, Mosby, what made thee murder him?
FRANKLIN
  Study not for an answer, look not down.
  His purse and girdle found at thy bed's head
  Witness sufficiently thou didst the deed.   15
  It bootless is to swear thou didst it not.
MOSBY
  I hired Black Will and Shakebag, ruffians both,
  And they and I have done this murd'rous deed.
  But wherefore stay we? Come and bear me hence.
FRANKLIN
  Those ruffians shall not escape. I will up to London   20
  And get the Council's warrant to apprehend them.
                                   Exeunt

13 *study not* do not try to invent
14 *girdle* belt (to carry the purse)
16 *bootless* useless, pointless

4-6 It was popularly believed that the corpse of a murdered man bled in the
    presence of his killer. Cf. *Richard III,* I.ii, 55–61.
17 – 19 Sturgess points out that it was, in fact, Greene who did the hiring at
    Alice's suggestion and with her money, and he suggests that this claim by
    Mosby is 'either an error of the playwright or a device by the playwright to
    cover Greene's absence.' As Wine observes, however, Mosby's confession
    'stems from a desperate awareness that the game is up. L19 makes it obvious
    that he wants the whole affair quickly over with.' He displays the same attitude
    in Scene XVIII (see 1.13 and 1.35).

Scene XVII

Here enters [BLACK] WILL

BLACK WILL
  Shakebag, I hear, hath taken sanctuary;
  But I am so pursued with hues and cries
  For petty robberies that I have done
  That I can come unto no sanctuary.
  Therefore must I in some oyster-boat   5
  At last be fain to go aboard some hoy,
  And so to Flushing. There is no staying here.
  At Sittingburgh the watch was like to take me,
  And, had I not with my buckler covered my head
  And run full blank at all adventures,   10
  I am sure I had ne'er gone further than that place,
  For the constable had twenty warrants to apprehend me;
  Besides that, I robbed him and his man once at Gadshill.
  Farewell, England; I'll to Flushing now.

                                    Exit [BLACK] WILL

Scene XVIII

Here enters the MAYOR, MOSBY, ALICE, MICHAEL
SUSAN, *and* BRADSHAW [*and the* WATCH]

MAYOR
  Come, make haste, and bring away the prisoners.
BRADSHAW
  Mistress Arden, you are now going to God,
  And I am by the law condemned to die
  About a letter I brought from Master Greene.
  I pray you, Mistress Arden, speak the truth: 5
  Was I ever privy to your intent or no?

6 *hoy* small boat used to carry passengers and goods
8 *like* likely
10 *full . . .adventures* headlong whatever the outcome

4 *About* on account of
6 *privy to* aware of

5–7 Faversham was renowned for its oyster beds, particularly by the Dutch, who
  traded regularly with the town.
13 *Gadshill* 'A hill on the road from London to Rochester' (Sugden). The scene of
  Falstaff's famous encounter with the 'rogues in buckram' (*1 Henry IV*, II.iv.).
  See also VII, 18n., above.

ALICE

What should I say? You brought me such a letter,
But I dare swear thou knewest not the contents.
Leave now to trouble me with worldly things,
And let me meditate upon my Saviour Christ,   10
Whose blood must save me for the blood I shed.

MOSBY

How long shall I live in this hell of grief?
Convey me from the presence of that strumpet.

ALICE

Ah, but for thee I had never been strumpet.
What cannot oaths and protestations do   15
When men have opportunity to woo?
I was too young to sound thy villainies,
But now I find it, and repent too late.

SUSAN

Ah, gentle brother, wherefore should I die?
I knew not of it till the deed was done.   20

MOSBY

For thee I mourn more than for myself,
But let it suffice I cannot save thee now.

MICHAEL

And if your brother and my mistress
Had not promised me you in marriage,
I had ne'er given consent to this foul deed.   25

MAYOR

Leave to accuse each other now,
And listen to the sentence I shall give:
Bear Mosby and his sister to London straight,
Where they in Smithfield must be executed;
Bear Mistress Arden unto Canterbury,   30
Where her sentence is she must be burnt;
Michael and Bradshaw in Faversham must suffer death.

ALICE

Let my death make amends for all my sins.

MOSBY

Fie upon women! — this shall be my song.
But bear me hence, for I have lived too long.   35

9 *Leave* cease
17 *sound* fathom
28 *straight* immediately

---

29 *Smithfield* 'An open space, East of the Tower of London just outside the city
walls. It was a haunt of riverside thieves, and was often used as the place for
their execution' (Sugden).

SUSAN
Seeing no hope on earth, in heaven is my hope.
MICHAEL
Faith, I care not, seeing I die with Susan.
BRADSHAW
My blood be on his head that gave the sentence!
MAYOR
To speedy execution with them all!   *Exeunt*

Epilogue

Here enters FRANKLIN

FRANKLIN
Thus have you seen the truth of Arden's death.
As for the ruffians, Shakebag and Black Will,
The one took sanctuary, and being sent for out,
Was murdered in Southwark as he passed
To Greenwich where the Lord Protector lay.   5
Black Will was burnt in Flushing on a stage;
Greene was hanged at Osbridge in Kent;
The painter fled, and how he died we know not.
But this above the rest is to be noted:
Arden lay murdered in that plot of ground   10
Which he by force and violence held from Reede;
And in the grass his body's print was seen
Two years and more after the deed was done.
Gentlemen, we hope you'll pardon this naked tragedy,
Wherein no filed points are foisted in   15
To make it gracious to the ear or eye;
For simple truth is gracious enough,
And needs no other points of glozing stuff.   [*Exit*]

---

6 *stage* scaffold
14 *naked* plain, straightforward
18 *glozing* specious

---

7 *Osbridge* i.e., Ospringe, 'a village in Kent, a mile or so South-West of Faversham' (Sugden).

15 *filed points* rhetorical figures. See Ousby for the view that far from being 'wholly conventional' or a 'mere formula', the 'playwright is warning us that rather than functioning as graceful adornment, "filed points" can be as deadly as dagger points.'

APPENDIX

From Holinshed's *Chronicles of England, Scotland and Ireland*
(Second Edition, 1587, 3 vols in 2, Vol. III, pp.1062-1066).

<table>
<tr><td>
1551
Anno Reg. 5.

Arden murdered.

Arden described.

Love and lust.

A pair of silver dice work much mischief.

Arden winketh at his wife's lewdness, and why!

Arden's wife attempteth means to make away her husband.

Arden is poisoned by his wife but recovereth.
</td><td>
About this time there was, at Faversham in Kent, a gentleman named Arden most cruelly murdered and slain by the procurement of his own wife. The which murder, for the horribleness thereof (although otherwise it may seem to be but a private matter, and therefore, as it were, impertinent to this history), I have thought good to set it forth somewhat at large, having the instructions delivered to me by them that used some diligence to gather the true understanding of the circumstances. This Arden was a man of a tall and comely personage, and matched in marriage with a gentle-woman young, tall and well favoured of shape and countenance, who chancing to fall in familiarity with one Mosby (a tailor by occupation, a black swart man, servant to the Lord North), it happened this Mosby, upon some misliking, to fall out with her. But she, being desirous to be in favour with him again, sent him a pair of silver dice by one Adam Fowle, dwelling at the Flower-de-Luce in Faversham.

After which he resorted to her again, and oftentimes lay in Arden's house, insomuch that within two years after he obtained such favour at her hands that he lay with her, or, as they term it, kept her, in abusing her body. And although (as it was said), Master Arden perceived right well their mutual familiarity to be much greater than their honesty, yet because he would not offend her and so lose the benefit which he hoped to gain at some of her friends hands in bearing with her lewdness, which he might have lost if he should have fallen out with her, he was contented to wink at her filthy disorder, and both permitted and also invited Mosby very often to lie in his house. And thus it continued a good space before any practice was begun by them against Master Arden. She, at length, inflamed in love with Mosby, and loathing her husband, wished and after practised the means how to hasten his end.

There was a painter dwelling in Faversham who had skill of poisons, as was reported. She therefore demanded of him whether it were true that he had such skill in that feat or not, and he denied not but that he had indeed. 'Yea,' said she, 'but I would have such a one made as should have most vehement and speedy operation to dispatch the eater thereof.' 'That can I do,' quoth he, and forthwith made her such a one, and willed her to put it into the bottom of a porringer and then after to pour milk on it; which circumstance she forgetting, did clean contrary, putting in the milk first, and afterward the poison. Now Master Arden purposing that day to ride to Canterbury, his wife brought him his breakfast, which was
</td></tr>
</table>

104

wont to be milk and butter. He, having received a spoonful or two or the milk, misliked the taste and colour thereof, and said to his wife, 'Mistress Alice, what milk have you given me here?' Wherewithal she tilted it over with her hand, saying, 'I ween nothing can please you.' Then he took horse and rode to Canterbury, and by the way fell into extreme purging upwards and downwards, and so escaped for that time.

After this, his wife fell in acquaintance with one Greene of Faversham, from which Greene Master Arden had wrested a piece of ground on the backside of the Abbey of Faversham, and there had blows and great threats passed betwixt them about that matter. Therefore she, knowing that Greene hated *She deviseth* her husband, began to practise with him how to make him *another way to* away, and concluded that if he could get any that that would *dispatch her* kill him, he should have ten pounds for a reward. This *husband Arden.* Greene, having doings for his master—Sir Anthony Ager—had occasion to go up to London where his master then lay, and having some charge up with him, desired one Bradshaw, a goldsmith of Faversham that was his neighbour, to accompany him to Gravesend, and he would content him for his pains. This Bradshaw, being a very honest man, was content, and rode with him. And when they came to Rainham Down they chanced to see three or four servingmen that were coming from Leeds, and therewith Bradshaw espied coming *A notorious* up the hill from Rochester one Black Will, a terrible cruel ruf- *murdering* fian with a sword and buckler, and another with a great staff *ruffian.* on his neck.

Then said Bradshaw to Greene, 'We are happy that here com- eth some company from Leeds, for here cometh up against us *Mark how the* as murdering a knave as any is in England. If it were not for *devil will not let* them we might chance hardly to escape without loss of our *his organs or* money and lives.' 'Yea,' thought Greene, as he after confess- *instruments let* ed, 'such a one is for my purpose,' and therefore asked, *slip either* 'Which is he?' 'Yonder is he,' quoth Bradshaw, 'the same *occasion or* that hath the sword and buckler: his name is Black Will.' *opportunity to* 'How know you that?' said Greene. Bradshaw answered, 'I *commit most* knew him at Boulogne, where we both served. He was a *heinous* soldier, and I was Sir Richard Cavendish's man, and there he *wickedness.* committed many robberies and heinous murders on such as travelled betwixt Boulogne and France.'

By this time the other company of servingmen came to them, and they all going together met with Black Will and his fellow. The servingmen knew Black Will and, saluting him, *A desperate* demanded of him whither he went. He answered, 'By His *villain.* blood!' (for his use was to swear almost at every word), 'I know not, nor care not, but set up my staff, and even as it falleth I go.' 'If thou,' quoth they, 'wilt go back again to Gravesend, we will give thee thy supper.' 'By His blood!' said he, 'I care not. I am content; have with you.' And so he returned again with them. Then Black Will took acquain-

tance of Bradshaw, saying, 'Fellow Bradshaw, how dost
thou?' Bradshaw, unwilling to renew acquaintance or to have
aught to do with so shameless a ruffian, said, 'Why, do ye
know me?' 'Yea, that I do,' quoth he. 'Did not we serve in
Boulogne together?' 'But ye must pardon me,' quoth Bradshaw, 'for I have forgotten you.'

An honest man is ashamed to renew old acquaintance with a knave.

Then Greene talked with Black Will, and said, 'When ye
have supped, come to mine host's house at such a sign and I
will give you the sack and sugar.' 'By His blood!' said he, 'I
thank you. I will come and take it I warrant you.' According
to his promise he came, and there they made good cheer.
Then Black Will and Greene went and talked apart from
Bradshaw, and there concluded together that if he would kill
Master Arden he should have ten pounds for his labour.
Then he answered, 'By His wounds! That I will if I may
know him.' 'Marry, tomorrow in Paul's I will show him
thee,' said Greene. Then they left their talk, and Greene bade
him go home to his host's house. Then Greene wrote a letter
to Mistress Arden, and among other things put in these
words: 'We have got a man for our purpose; we may thank
my brother Bradshaw'. Now Bradshaw, not knowing
anything of this, took the letter of him, and in the morning
departed home again, and delivered the letter to Mistress
Arden. And Greene and Black Will went up to London at the
tide.

The match made to murder Arden.

Simplicity abused.

At the time appointed, Greene showed Black Will Master
Arden walking in Paul's. Then said Black Will, 'What is he
that goeth after him?' 'Marry,' said Greene, 'one of his men.'
By His blood!' said Black Will, 'I will kill them both.' 'Nay,'
said Greene, 'do not so, for he is of counsel with us in this
matter.' 'By His blood,' said he, 'I care not for that, I will kill
them both.' 'Nay,' said Greene, 'in any wise do not so.' Then
Black Will thought to have killed Master Arden in Paul's
churchyard, but there were so many gentlemen that accompanied him to dinner that he missed of his purpose. Greene
showed all this talk to Master Arden's man, whose name was
Michael, which ever after stood in doubt of Black Will lest he
should kill him. The cause that this Michael conspired with
the rest against his master was for that it was determined that
he should marry a kinswoman of Mosby's.

Black Will maketh no conscience of bloodshed and murder.

Why Arden's man conspired with the rest to kill his master.

After this, Master Arden lay at a certain parsonage which he
held in London, and therefore his man Michael and Greene
agreed that Black Will should come in the night to the parsonage, where he should find the doors left open that he
might come in and murder Master Arden. This Michael, having his master to bed, left open the doors according to the appointment. His master, then being in bed, asked him if he had
shut fast the doors, and he said, 'Yea.' But yet, afterwards,
fearing lest Black Will would kill him as well as his master,
after he was in bed himself, he rose again and shut the doors,
bolting them fast, so that Black Will will coming thither and

One murdering mind mistrusting another do hinder the action whereabout they agreed.

finding the doors shut, departed, being disappointed at that time. The next day, Black Will came to Greene in a great chafe, swearing and staring because he was so deceived, and with many terrible oaths threatened to kill Master Arden's man first, wheresoever he met him. 'No,' said Greene, 'do not so. I will first know the cause of shutting the doors.'

Then Greene met and talked with Arden's man, and asked of him why he did not leave open the doors according to his promise. 'Marry,' said Michael, 'I will show you the cause. My master yesternight did that he never did before, for after I was *The fourth* in bed he rose up and shut the doors, and in the morning *attempt to make* rated me for leaving them unshut.' And herewith Greene and *Arden away* Black Will were pacified. Arden being ready to go *disappointed.* homewards, his maid came to Greene and said, 'This night will my master go down.' Whereupon it was agreed that Black Will should kill him on Rainham Down. When Master Arden came to Rochester his man, still fearing that Black Will would kill him with his master, pricked his horse of purpose and made him to halt, to the end he might protract the time and tarry behind. His master asked him why his horse halted. He said, 'I know not.' 'Well,' quoth his master, 'when ye come at the smith here before, between Rochester and the hill-foot over against Cheetham, remove his shoe and search him, and then come after me.' So Master Arden rode on, and *Black Will* ere he came at the place where Black Will lay in wait for him *misseth his* there overtook him diverse gentlemen of his acquaintance *purpose.* who kept him company, so that Black Will missed here also of his purpose.

After that Master Arden was come home, he sent, as he usually did, his man to Sheppey, to Sir Thomas Cheiny, then Lord Warden of the Cinque Ports, about certain business, and at his coming away he had a letter delivered sent by Sir Thomas Cheiny to his master. When he came home, his mistress took the letter and kept it, willing her man to tell his master that he had a letter delivered him by Sir Thomas Cheiny and that he had lost it, adding that he thought it best that his master should go the next morning to Sir Thomas, because he knew not the matter. He said he would, and therefore he willed his man to be stirring betimes. In this meanwhile, Black Will and one George Shakebag, his companion, were kept in a store-house of Sir Anthony Ager's at Preston by Greene's ap- *Arden's wife* pointment, and thither came Mistress Arden to see him, br- *visiteth,* inging and sending him meat and drink many times. He, *succoureth,* therefore, lurking there and watching some opportunity for *emboldeneth, and* his purpose, was willed in any wise to be up early in the mor- *directeth Black* ning to lie in wait for Master Arden in a certain broom close *Will, &c. how to* betwixt Faversham and the ferry (which close he needs must *accomplish his* pass), there to do his feat. Now Black Will stirred in the mor- *bloody purpose.* ning betimes, but missed the way and tarried in a wrong place.

Master Arden and his man coming on their way early in the
morning towards Shorlow, where Sir Thomas Cheiny lay, as
they were almost come to the broom close, his man, always
fearing that Black Will would kill him with his master, feign-
ed that he had lost his purse. 'Why,' said his master, 'thou
foolish knave, couldst thou not look to thy purse but lose it?
What was in it?' 'Three pounds,' said he. 'Why then, go thy
ways back again like a knave,' said his master, 'and seek it, for
being so early as it is there is no man stirring, and therefore
thou mayest be sure to find it, and then come and overtake me
at the ferry.' But nevertheless, by reason that Black Will
lost his way, Master Arden escaped once again. At that time,
Black Will yet thought he should have been sure to have met
him homewards, but whether that some of the Lord
Warden's men accompanied him back to Faversham, or that
being in doubt, for that it was late to go through the broom
close, and therefore took another way, Black Will was disappointed then also.

But now Saint Valentine's fair being at hand, the conspirators
thought to dispatch their devilish intention at that time.
Mosby minded to pick some quarrel to Master Arden at the
fair to fight with him, for, he said, he could not find it in his
heart to murder a gentleman in that sort as his wife wished,
although she had made a solemn promise to him, and he again
to her, to be in all points as man and wife together, and
thereupon they both received the sacrament on a Sunday at
London, openly in a church there. But this device to fight
with him would not serve, for Master Arden, both then and at
other times, had been greatly provoked by Mosby to fight
with him, but he would not. Now Mosby had a sister that
dwelt in a tenement of Master Arden's, near to his house in
Faversham, and on the fair even, Black Will was sent for to
come thither; and Greene bringing him thither met there
with Mistress Arden, accompanied with Michael, her man,
and one of her maids. There were also Mosby and George
Shakebag, and there they devised to have killed him in manner as afterwards he was. But yet Mosby at the first would not
agree to that cowardly murdering of him, but in a fury flung
away, and went up the Abbey street towards the Flower-de-
Luce, the house of the aforenamed Adam Fowle, where he
did often host. But before he came thither, now at this time, a
messenger overtook him that was sent from Mistress Arden,
desiring him of all loves to come back again to help to accomplish the matter he knew of. Hereupon he returned to her
again, and at his coming back she fell down upon her knees to
him and besought him to go through with the matter, as if he
loved her he would be content to do; sith, as she had divers
times told him, he needed not to doubt, for there was not any
that would care for his death, nor make any great enquiry for
them that should dispatch him.

Thus, she being earnest with him, at length he was contented

Note here the force of fear and a troubled conscience.

Black Will yet again disappointed.

A prepensed quarrel against Arden by the conspirators.

Arden's wife Black Will, & the knot of villains meet and conclude upon their former prepensed mischief.

O Importunate & bloody minded strumpet!

to agree unto that horrible device, and thereupon they conveyed Black Will into Master Arden's house, putting him into a closet at the end of his parlour. Before this they had sent out of the house all the servants, those excepted which were privy to the devised murder. Then went Mosby to the doors, and there stood in a night-gown of silk girded about him, and this was betwixt six and seven of the clock at night. Master Arden, having been at a neighbour's house of his named Dumpkin, and having cleared certain reckonings betwixt them, came home, and finding Mosby standing at the door asked him if it were supper-time. 'I think not,' quoth Mosby, 'it is not yet ready.' 'Then let us go and play a game at the tables in the mean season,' said Master Arden. And so they went straight into the parlour, and as they came by through the hall his wife was walking there, and Master Arden said, 'How now, Mistress Alice?' But she made small answer to him. In the meantime, one chained the wicket door of the entry. When they came into the parlour, Mosby sat down on the bench, having his face toward the place where Black Will stood. Then Michael, Master Arden's man, stood at his master's back, holding a candle in his hand to shadow Black Will, that Arden might by no means perceive him coming forth. In their play, Mosby said thus (which seemed to be the watch-word for Black Will's coming forth): 'Now may I take you, sir, if I will.' 'Take me?' quoth Master Arden. 'Which way?' With that, Black Will stepped forth and cast a towel about his neck, so to stop his breath and strangle him. Then Mosby, having at his girdle a pressing-iron of fourteen pounds weight, struck him on the head with the same, so that he fell down and gave a great groan, insomuch that they thought he had been killed.

Then they bare him away to lay him in the countinghouse, and as they were about to lay him down, the pangs of death coming on him, he gave a great groan and stretched himself. And then Black Will gave him a great gash in the face and so killed him out of hand, laid him along, took the money out of his purse and the rings from his fingers, and then coming out of the countinghouse said, 'Now the feat is done, give me my money.' So Mistress Arden gave him ten pounds, and he coming to Greene had a horse of him, and so rode his ways. After that Black Will was gone, Mistress Arden came into the countinghouse and with a knife gave him seven or eight pricks into the breast. Then they made clean the parlour, took a clout and wiped where it was bloody, and strewed again the rushes that were shuffled with struggling, and cast the clout with which they wiped the blood and the knife that was bloody, wherewith she had wounded her husband, into a tub by the well's side, where afterwards both the same clout and knife were found. Thus this wicked woman, with her 'complices, most shamefully murdered her own husband, who most entirely loved her all his lifetime. Then she sent for two

The practice to kill Arden is now set abroach.

Here the confederates join their practices.

The watch-word to the principal murderer.

Arden slain outright.

Black Will receiveth ten pounds for his reward of Arden's wife for murdering her husband.

Londoners to supper, the one named Prune and the other Cole, that were grocers, which before the murder was committed were bidden to supper. When they came she said, 'I marvel where Master Arden is. We will not tarry for him, come ye and sit down, for he will not be long.' Then Mosby's sister was sent for. She came and sat down, and so they were merry.

Mark what a countenance of innocence and ignorance she bore after the murdering of her husband.

After supper, Mistress Arden caused her daughter to play on the virginals, and they danced, and she with them, and so seemed to protract time, as it were, till Master Arden should come. And she said, 'I marvel where he is so long. Well, he will come anon, I am sure. I pray you, in the meanwhile let us play a game at the tables.' But the Londoners said they must go to their host's house or else they should be shut out at doors, and so, taking their leave, departed. When they were gone, the servants that were not privy to the murder were sent abroad into the town, some to seek their master and some of other errands, all saving Michael and a maid, Mosby's sister, and one of Mistress Arden's own daughters. Then they

The workers of this mischief carry out Arden slain into the field.

took the dead body and carried it out to lay it in a field next to the churchyard and joining to his garden wall, through the which he went to the church. In the meantime it began to snow, and when they came to the garden gate they remembered that they had forgotten the key, and one went in for it, and finding it, at length brought it, opened the gate, and carried the corpse into the same field, as it were ten paces from the garden gate, and laid him down on his back straight in his night-gown, with his slippers on, and between one of his slippers and his foot a long rush or two remained. When they had thus laid him down, they returned the same way they came through the garden gate into the house.

They being returned thus back again into the house the doors were opened and the servants returned home that had been

This she did to colour her wickedness which by no means was excuseable.

sent abroad, and being now very late, she sent forth her folks again to make enquiry for him in divers places, namely among the best in the town where he was wont to be, who made answer that they could tell nothing of him. Then she began to make an outcry, and said, 'Never woman had such neighbours as I have,' and herewith wept, insomuch that her neighbours came in and found her making great lamentation, pretending to marvel what was become of her husband. Whereupon the mayor and others came to make search for

Arden a covetous man and a preferer of his private profit before common gain.

him. The fair was wont to be kept partly in the town and partly in the Abbey, but Arden, for his own private lucre and covetous gain, had this present year procured it to be wholly kept within the Abbey ground which he had purchased, and so reaping all the gains to himself and bereaving the town of that portion which was wont to come to the inhabitants, got many a bitter curse. The mayor, going about the fair in this search, at length came to the ground where Arden lay, and as it happened, Prune the grocer getting sight of him first said, 'Stay, for methink I see one lie here.' And so they, looking and beholding the body, found that it was Master Arden lying

Arden's dead body is descried by one of his acquaintance.

there thoroughly dead, and viewing diligently the manner of his body and hurts, found the rushes sticking in his slippers, and, marking further, espied certain footsteps, by reason of the snow, betwixt the place where he lay and the garden door. Then the mayor commanded every man to stay, and herewith appointed some to go about and come in at the inner side of the house through the garden as the way lay, to the place where Master Arden's dead body did lie, who all the way as they came perceived footings still before them in the snow;

Footsteps all alongst from the dead body of Arden to his dwelling house.

and so it appeared plainly that he was brought along that way from the house through the garden and so into the field where he lay. Then the mayor and his company that were with him went into the house, and knowing her evil demeanour in times past examined her of the matter. But she defied them and said, 'I would you should know I am no such woman.'

A piece of Arden's hair and his blood spilt in the house espied, as also a bloody knife and a clout found.

Then they examined her servants, and in the examination—by reason of a piece of his hair and blood found near to the house in the way by the which they carried him forth, and likewise by the knife with which she had thrust him into the breast, and the clout wherewith they wiped the blood away which they found in the tub into the which the same were thrown—they all confessed the matter, and herself beholding her husband's blood said, 'Oh, the blood of God help, for this blood have I shed.'

Then were they all attached and committed to prison, and the mayor with others went presently to the Flower-de-Luce where they found Mosby in bed. And as they came towards him they espied his hose and purse stained with some of Master Arden's blood, and when he asked what they meant by their coming in such sort they said, 'See, here ye may

Some of Arden's blood upon Mosby's purse.

The principals of his murder fled away.

understand wherefore by these tokens,' showing him the blood on his hose and purse. Then he confessed the deed, and so he and all the other that had conspired the murder were apprehended and laid in prison, except Greene, Black Will, and the painter, which painter and George Shakebag, that was also fled before, were never heard of. Shortly were the sessions kept at Faversham, where all the prisoners were arraigned and condemned. And thereupon being examined whether they had any other 'complices, Mistress Arden accused Brad-

Bradshaw as unjustly accused as his simplicity was shamefully abused.

shaw upon occasion of the letter sent by Greene from Gravesend (as before ye have heard), which words had none other meaning but only by Bradshaw's describing of Black Will's qualities, Greene judged him a meet instrument for the execution of their pretended murder. Whereunto, notwithstanding (as Greene confessed at his death certain years after), this Bradshaw was never made privy, howbeit, he was upon this occasion of Mistress Arden immediately sent for to the sessions and indicted, and declaration made against him as a procurer of Black Will to kill Master Arden, which proceeded wholly by misunderstanding of the words contained in the letter which he brought from Greene.

Then he desired to talk with the persons condemned, and his request was granted. He therefore demanded of them if they knew him or ever had any conversation with him, and they all said no. Then the letter being showed and read, he declared

Innocence no bar against execution.

the very truth of the matter and upon what occasion he told Greene of Black Will. Nevertheless, he was condemned and suffered. These condemned persons were diversely executed in sundry places; for Michael, Master Arden's man, was hanged in chains at Faversham, and one of the maids was

Note how these malefactors suffered punishment.

burnt there, pitifully bewailing her case, and cried out on her mistress that had brought her to this end, for the which she would never forgive her. Mosby and his sister were hanged in Smithfield at London. Mistress Arden was burned at Canterbury the four and twentieth of March. Greene came again certain years after, was apprehended, condemned, and hanged in chains in the highway between Ospring and Boughton-against-Faversham. Black Will was burnt on a scaffold at

Black Will burnt at Flushing

Flushing in Zealand. Adam Fowle, that dwelt at the Flower-de-Luce in Faversham was brought into trouble about this matter, and carried up to London with his legs bound under the horse's belly, and committed to prison in the Marshalsea, for that Mosby was heard to say, 'Had it not been for Adam Fowle, I had not come to this trouble,' meaning that the bringing of the silver dice for a token to him from Mistress Arden, as ye have heard, occasioned him to renew familiarity with her again. But when the matter was thoroughly ripped up, and that Mosby had cleared him, protesting that he was never of knowledge in any behalf to the murder, the man's innocence preserved him.

A wonder touching the print of Arden's dead body two years after he was slain.

This one thing seemed very strange and notable touching Master Arden, that in the place where he was laid, being dead, all the proportion of his body might be seen two years after and more so plain as could be, for the grass did not grow where his body had touched, but between his legs, between his arms, and about the hollowness of his neck, and round about his body; and where his legs, arms, head, or any other part of his body had touched, no grass growed at all of all that time, so that many strangers came in that meantime, beside the townsmen, to see the print of his body there on the ground in that field, which field he had (as some have reported), most cruelly taken from a woman that had been a widow to one Cooke, and after married to one Richard Read, a mariner, to the great hindrance of her and her husband, the said Read; for they had long enjoyed it by a lease which they had of it for many years, not then expired. Nevertheless, he got it from them, for the which the said Read's wife not only exclaimed against him in shedding many a salt tear, but also cursed him most bitterly even to his face, wishing many a vengeance to light upon him, and that all the world might wonder on him. Which was thought then to come to pass

God heareth the tears of the oppressed and taketh vengeance: note an example in Arden.

when he was thus murdered and lay in that field from midnight till the morning, and so all that day, being the fair day till night; all the which day there were many hundreds of people came wondering about him. And thus far touching this horrible and heinous murder of Master Arden.